OTHER BOOKS BY DONALD C. FARBER

Producing on Broadway
Actor's Guide: What You Should Know
About the Contracts You Sign
Producing, Financing and Distributing Film
(with co-author Paul A. Baumgarten)
Producing Theatre: A Comprehensive Legal and Business Guide

FROM OPTION TO OPENING

A Guide to Producing Plays Off-Broadway

FROM OPTION TO OPENING

A Guide to Producing Plays Off-Broadway

Donald C. Farber

Fourth Edition, Revised

Limelight Editions
New York

First Limelight Edition October 1988
Copyright © 1968, 1970, 1977 by Donald C. Farber

All rights reserved under international and Pan-American Copyright Convention. Published in the United States by Proscenium Publishers Inc., New York, and simultaneously in Canada by Fitzhenry & Whiteside, Limited, Toronto.

Library of Congress Cataloging-in-Publication Data
Farber, Donald C.
    From option to opening: a guide to producing plays Off-Broadway/ Donald C. Farber.—Rev. and updated ed., 1st Limelight ed.
    p.   cm.
    ISBN 0-87910-114-8: $12.95
    1. Theater—Production and direction. 2. Off-Broadway theater. I. Title.
PN2291.F3 1988
792'.0232—dc19   88-9092
                                                                 CIP

for . . .
Annie
Patty
Seth
and the new additions
since last publication
Justin
Miranda
Nef

I want to express my
special thanks to
George Elmer for his
helpful assistance
with the budgets and
related items.

Contents

PREFACE TO THE FOURTH EDITION   xi
ACKNOWLEDGMENTS   xiii
INTRODUCTION   xv

1 OPTIONING A PROPERTY   3
  Warranties and Representations   4
  Length of the Option   4
  Option Cost   5
  Play Cost (Royalties)   6
  What the Option Buys   7
  What an Option Conditionally Buys   8
    Right to Tour   8
    English Production   10
    Right to Move to Broadway   11
    Subsidiary Rights   11
  Billing Credits   15
    Billing Box   17
  House Seats   17
  Authors' Approvals   17
  Arbitration   18
  Assignability of Option   18
  Option of First Refusal   19
  Buyer's Market   19
  Adaptations   20
    Merger of Rights   20

Basic Work—Copyright Ownership   21
Royalties for Basic Work   21
Basic Work Option Fee (Adaptations)   22
The Adaptor   22

2 CO-PRODUCTION AGREEMENTS   25
Front Money   26
Associate Producer—Money   28

3 THE PRODUCING COMPANY   31
Partnership or Corporation   31
Limited Liability   31
Tax Benefits   32
Corporation As a Partner   33
The Limited Partnership   34
How and What Is Limited   34
Legal Publication (Theatrical Exception)   35
Limited Partnership Agreement Form   36
Profit Sharing   36
Budget and Capitalization   37
Abandonment   38
Payment of Profits   38
Return of Profits to Company   39
Producer's Fee and Cash Office Charge   39
Bonds and Bond Deals   40
Overcalls and Loans   42
Option Provisions in Agreement   42
Termination of Partnership   42
Miscellaneous   43

4 RAISING THE MONEY   45
Budgets   45
Typical Budgets (Examples)   47
Backers' Auditions   47
The Securities and Exchange Commission   49
Filing for an Exemption   51
Offering Circular   51
The Attorney General   53
Investment Procedure   54
Starting the Company   55

5 OBTAINING A THEATRE 57
    Advance Deposit 58
    Four-Wall Contract 58
    Lease or License 58
    Run of the Show and Moving 59
    Stop Clause 60
    Payment of Rent 60
    Theatre License and Rehearsals 61
    Equity Requirements 61
    Theatre Deposit 62
    Maintenance and Concessions 62
    Advertising 62
    Removal at End of Run—and House Seats 63
    Insurance 63
    Assignability 64
    Location 64
    Bargaining 65
    Variety of Theatres 65

6 CAST, CREW, AND PERSONNEL 67
    The Director 67
    Sample Breakdown of Fees 69
    The Cast 70
        The Actors' Equity Association Contract 70
    The Stage Manager 72
    Set, Costume, and Lighting Designs 73
    Press Agent 75
    Advertising Agency 76
    General Manager 76
    Company Manager 77
    Accountants and Accountings 78
    Attorney 79

7 MUSICALS 81
    Original Cast Album 82
    Publisher 83
    Musicians 84
    Arrangements and Music Preparation 84
    Choreographer 85
    Musical Director 86

8 REHEARSALS, OPEN, RUN, OR CLOSE   87
    Rehearsals   88
    Previews   88
    Opening Night   89
    Reviews   89
    Party   90
    After Opening Night   90
    Scaling the House, Twofers, Discount Tickets   93
    Middle Theatres in New York   94

9 REPERTORIES, CHILDREN'S THEATRE, AND
    OFF-OFF-BROADWAY   97
    Repertory Company   97
    Children's Theatre   98
    Off-Off-Broadway   99

10 VITALLY IMPORTANT ODDS AND END   103
    The Art of Negotiation   103
    Conflicts of Interest   106
    Package Deals   107
    The League of Off-Broadway Theatres and Producers   107
    Ethics—Honesty   108
    Good Producing   109

APPENDICES   111
    Appendix A: Option Agreement   113
    Appendix B: Co-Production Agreement   127
    Appendix C: Budget for a Musical   137
              Budget for a Musical Review (Cabaret)   145
    Appendix D: Offering Circular   151
    Appendix E: Budget for a Middle Theatre   177

Preface to the Fourth Edition

FOURTH EDITION, I CAN'T BELIEVE IT! You have to know that of all the books that I have written, and it's been a few, this is my favorite. When this was originally written, Off-Broadway was Off-Broadway, instead of a smaller version of Broadway in a different part of town.

Way back then, and we are talking about 1968, Jerry Orbach left *The Threepenny Opera* to play one of the leads in *The Fantasticks* and Sylvia Miles was wowing them in *The Balcony* at Circle in the Square (downtown, of course, because then that was the only Circle in the Square). David Ross was doing his Chekhov, Strindberg was at the Provincetown Playhouse, and actors were paid $25 a week, those that were lucky enough to be working.

Julius Monk's Upstairs at the Downstairs was *the* chic place in town, Bobby Short was knocking them dead in the lobby (yes, the lobby) of Max Gordon's (that was the original) Blue Angel, and Barbra Streisand was just being discovered in *I Can Get It for You Wholesale.* One of my clients brought the Maharishi Mahesh Yogi over here and presented him at the Felt Forum, and he put a lot of people to sleep. But he became a phenomenon, and I represented the organization while the phenomenon was at his height.

We ran to see theatre in barns, in attics, in warehouses, and in garages. The play was the thing. "Black" theatre was coming alive. I represented the New Lafayette Theatre and was fortunate enough to be part of this marvelous community theatre where Ed Bullins was the writer-in-residence and Bob MacBeth was the director. Whitman Mayo came out of that, as did Richard Wesley and Sonny Jim Gaines.

Those of us in the business then were trying to make some sense of it, and we were making agreements to serve the purposes of the parties at the time. It was a time of creativity, sensitivity, dedication, and devotion—yes, devotion to "the art." The only reason for making money then was to stay alive so that the play could open the next day.

I must confess my astonishment when I started rewriting this plain, simple "how to" and discovered that no matter how you slice it, it cannot any longer be that "plain" or that "simple."

I tried. And to the extent that I could, I attempted to keep the feeling and ambience of the original published in 1968. The problem with "plain and simple" is that back then my knowledge was fresh and naïve, and now the scene and I have both become a little jaded. So this book is a little more exact, and I hope a little more sophisticated, and perhaps a great deal more informative.

Bear in mind that there are no final dollar amounts of the union contracts discussed. This is a continuing problem, since even if the constantly variable terms have been updated for this edition, they may have become outdated soon after publication.

You may easily communicate with any respective union to obtain an updated contract. The budgets added are current budgets and reflect any changes to date. The basics set forth in this book are indeed "basics," and as I said, are applicable to most theatre.

I hope this book contributes to your better understanding of the theatre business and that it brings you as much pleasure as I had in writing it.

Donald C. Farber

New York City, 1988

Acknowledgments

Special thanks go to Mitchell Lapidus for his checking me on the tax advice, to Pam Markley for her ever willingness to help and her helping, and to Carol Solar-Caruso for her excellent typing and always pleasant disposition.

My associate, Deborah Gunset, has been most helpful, especially with the agreements, and for this I am grateful.

Jan Lurie, assistant to the publisher, has assisted in ways too numerous to mention, for which I am appreciative and thankful.

Thanks also to my editor, Alice Kenner, whose careful attention to detail is much appreciated.

I haven't forgotten that Ralph Pine of Drama Book Specialists started this all when he published the first edition of this, my first book. For this I am and always will be appreciative.

Big thanks to my present publisher, Mel Zerman, whose professionalism and enthusiasm for my work has made the often tedious job of revising and updating a pleasant experience, and for keeping this book alive.

Introduction

WHEN I WROTE THIS BOOK IN 1968, "Off-Broadway" was still in an early stage of development. Twenty years later, when I sat down to update the book, I realized that I liked what I had written in the Introduction to the first edition. So I want to duplicate it here as it was written then, with one minor exception. Rather than change the dollar amounts and references, I have indicated in parentheses the amounts and references that would be different now in the year 1988. In this way a comparison can be made that will indicate some of the changes that have taken place. I didn't follow this procedure with the rest of the book because it would have been too distracting. The rest of the book has been updated without any indication as to "what was" way back in 1968.

Off-Broadway producing is a business. In fact, it has become an important part of the business that there is no business like. It's difficult to measure the influence that Off-Broadway has had on our theatre. We do know, of course, that many of our important stars and prominent playwrights were first discovered in Off-Broadway productions. The influence of Off-Broadway extends even further, however, as Off-Broadway productions have actually influenced the direction and development of our theatre.

"I think it's not good enough for a Broadway production, so it probably should be done Off-Broadway," has been said often. What a gross error to assume that a play must be good for Broadway and something less than good for Off-Broadway.

There are distinctions between what should be done on Broadway and what should be done Off-Broadway, but it has nothing to do with the quality of the show. There are, for example, different markets. Some people will patronize Broadway shows who would never patronize an Off-Broadway show until it is a smash hit. The theatre-party groups are partial to Broadway productions. The expense-account executive entertains his out-of-town guests at a Broadway show. The student and progressive thinker may patronize an experimental Off-Broadway production. Usually Off-Broadway tickets are cheaper, so persons on a limited budget may think twice before they spend $45 or $50 ($10 in 1968 and $15 in 1977) for a Broadway show, but will only think once about spending almost half that amount for an Off-Broadway show. Some productions fare better in intimate surroundings. There are no intimate Broadway theatres in the same sense that the less than 299-seat Off-Broadway theatres are intimate.

Of course, it costs many times as much to produce a Broadway show than it does to produce an Off-Broadway show, but this should not be the determining factor as to where you produce the show. Different plays belong in different markets and raising money is a tough job whether its $5 million ($150,000 in 1968 and $200,000 in 1977) for a Broadway musical or $250,000 ($25,000 in 1968 and $40,000 in 1977) for an Off-Broadway play. (My, how times change.)

I like to quote the comedian Joe E. Lewis to my classes and to my clients. He used to say, "What good's happiness if it can't buy money?"

A successful Off-Broadway producer must have the unique combination of good creative judgment, taste, and business sense. Along with these qualities, the would-be producer must be able to raise capital for something in which he or she believes. The rewards for the producer of a successful Off-Broadway show can be large quantities of money, but this by itself is rarely enough incentive to result in a totally satisfactory production. There also may be aesthetic rewards that come from doing something one strongly believes in.

How do you start? How do you get the answers to the numerous questions that will confront you and plague you? Are you even aware of the questions that will need answering? I suspect that one could start working as an usher Off-Broadway, work oneself into the position of treasurer of the box office, and know a lot of things about how a production is handled without really knowing what the job of producing a theatrical play consists of. The only course that I know of on the hard business facts of Off-Broadway life is the one I teach on "Theatre

Producing" at the New School for Social Research, in New York City. This book can help, but no book can be the substitute for countless man-hours of experience.

Before proceeding further, we really ought to have some idea of what we mean by "Off-Broadway." Off-Broadway is defined as the Borough of Manhattan outside the area bounded by Fifth and Ninth Avenues, from Thirty-fourth Street to Fifty-sixth Street, and by Fifth Avenue to the Hudson River from Fifty-sixth Street to Seventy-second Street. An Off-Broadway theatre, in addition to being outside that area, can have no more than 499 seats. A "middle theatre" is a theatre within the Broadway area that seats no more than 499. If a theatre is outside the Broadway area, with 500 seats or more, it is neither an Off-Broadway theatre nor a middle theatre, but could be labeled an anomaly.

Just a word on the uniqueness of the Off-Broadway theatre scene before we start tackling the problems. It can be noted that Off-Broadway producing is unlike anything else in the world. If you are producing a Broadway show, in most areas there are some standards—certain well-defined, previously defined limits to your contractual experiences. In the Off-Broadway arena, the contractual arrangements are less well defined. For an example, if your are optioning a Broadway script, the Approved Production Contract (APC) negotiated by the Dramatists Guild, Inc., and the League of American Theatres and Producers provides a contract with minimum and maximum terms. Any amendments can only cover items omitted or clarify any terms that are vague. Not so Off-Broadway, where the range of option terms is variable. When this book was first published, there were fewer precedents, but through the years some precedents have been established that serve to narrow the range of the terms of the options.

When the negotiations between the Off-Broadway League and the Dramatists Guild, Inc., broke up many years ago, the Guild came out with it own version of a Minimum Basic Agreement for Off-Broadway. No one with any knowledge would think of using that contract, and it has had very little use through the years.

You will of necessity, as a producer, be confronted with a variety of legal problems and legal documents. It is intended here to discuss, in nonlegal language, problems that may come up for you, as it is a recognized fact that few Off-Broadway producers are attorneys. Whether any practicing attorneys should be producing Off-Broadway shows instead of doing what they're doing is a matter of conjecture.

This book is being written from the point of view of the producer and not from that of the author. No slight of authors is intended, for as a lawyer I represent authors as well as producers. It's just that this book is about how to produce an Off-Broadway play and not how to write an Off-Broadway play. I couldn't begin to tell anyone how to write a play, for this I don't know myself. If I did, I would probably be writing plays instead of books on how to produce plays.

I will attempt to define for you certain concepts, ideas, and terms that are indefinable by normal expected standards. What I want to do is discuss "specifics" in general. It will be impossible for me to pinpoint certain facts, but what I will have to do is to set broad limits within which your questions may fall. In doing this, it is not my purpose here to explore the rare or unusual. There is enough divergence—that is, enough distance—between the extremes on any given subject in Off-Broadway contracts without detailing the one in one thousand rarity that is outside even those limits. The purpose of this book must be to define the usual outer limits within which most Off-Broadway contracts and Off-Broadway experiences will fit, and at the same time to suggest what would be considered fair, reasonable, or not unusual, bearing in mind what is right for one person may be all wrong for another.

Although you will notice my almost constant use of such terms as *usually, not unusual, most of the time, frequently,* parties entering into an agreement may agree to anything as long as they do not violate any law or agree to something contrary to public policy. If investors in a show consent that the general partner may use the funds to purchase a Rolls-Royce for the partner's own use in furtherance of the production, then he or she may do so. Anything is possible. Our discussion will confine itself to what is usual rather than to what is possible.

The problems that will be faced by an Off-Broadway producer are in many ways similar to the problems of theatre producers throughout the country. The producer of a play for a university, community, or summer stock theatre will have to obtain the rights to do the play, will have to make arrangements with the investors, may have to satisfy the Securities and Exchange Commission, and do most of the other things that are outlined in detail in this book with reference to Off-Broadway producing. The minor details may be slightly different, but the basic concepts are the same.

FROM OPTION TO OPENING

A Guide to Producing Plays Off-Broadway

CHAPTER 1

Optioning a Property

THE FIRST THING THAT you must do as the producer of a play is to obtain a "property." *Property* is the word that is used for the play or other work you want to perform or have performed. The author or owner of the play will either represent him/herself or be represented by an agent or by an attorney. When we refer to an owner, we may be referring to someone other than the author, who may own the right to deal in the play, having inherited it or having purchased it. Unless otherwise specifically noted, all of the observations that refer to the author would be equally applicable to an owner of the play who is not the author.

On many occasions, I have been confronted by a client who has consulted me after already having signed a piece of paper he labeled an "option to produce an off-Broadway play." The client means well, he knows legal advice is necessary and he's now seeking it. Upon reading the "option," it becomes apparent that the client should have consulted an attorney *before* entering into the agreement. The option agreement contains no provision for subsidiary rights (these will be explained in detail later) nor does it make provision for a right to tour the show or to do an English production of the show, if it is later deemed advisable. An option agreement that does not get for the producer everything that he or she ought to have is not just bad for the producer personally but is also bad for the investors, and this could make it very difficult for the producer to raise the money to produce the play.

Therefore, before signing any agreements, the knowledgeable producer consults an attorney, who will then communicate with the author or the author's representative to discuss the various terms of the option. An option agreement is simply a grant of the right to produce a play, in exchange for a money payment to the author. The amount of money paid, the length of the option, what the money payment buys, are all variables—negotiable items—which will be defined precisely in the option agreement.

WARRANTIES AND REPRESENTATIONS

As the producer, you will want to make certain that the option to produce a play contains certain warranties and representations by the author or owner. In plain nonlegal language, this means simply that the author guarantees, assures, and even insures that what is being sold to you is owned by the author/owner. In the agreement it is stated that the person selling the rights of the play is someone who has acquired the rights to sell the play; that there have been no lawsuits that would endanger his or her ownership of the play; and that if it turns out that this person does not own the play and you are damaged as a result, this person will reimburse you to the extent that you have suffered from his or her misrepresentations. The warranties clause of an option agreement usually makes reference to the copyright ownership by the author or owner, and states the date and number of the copyright registration.

LENGTH OF THE OPTION

Off-Broadway options can run for various terms; however, it is not unusual to have an option for a one-year period that can be extended for an additional one year upon payment of an additional sum of money. It then may be extended for an additional six months after that for still an additional sum of money. A one-year option means that the play must open before a paying audience on or before one year from the date of the option agreement. Sometimes an option will be for a one-year period with the right to extend the option for an additional six months. It used to be widely believed that an Off-Broadway show would have a difficult time opening during the summer months. This is no longer the case and most knowledgeable persons believe a show can open anytime during the year, although right around Christmas may be iffy. What's more important is putting on a good show.

OPTION COST

In exchange for the right to produce the play to open on or before a specific date, a producer pays a sum of money that is usually considered to be an advance against royalties. The term *advance against royalties* means exactly what it sounds like. This payment, being an advance against royalties, means that the amount of the payment is deducted from the first royalties earned by the author.

Determined as it is by a number of factors, the amount of the option payment will vary. A well-known playwright who has many Broadway productions to his credit will of course demand, and receive, a larger option payment than an unknown author who has never had a play produced. In all events, the author's motivation, how badly he or she wants to see the play produced, the rapport between the producer and the author, the existence of other producers who may be anxious to produce the play, and other such factors can affect the amount of money that will be demanded, and paid, for the option. A one-year option would probably cost on either side of $750, and it is often provided that the payments will be made with $350 due on signing of the option and $400 six months after the signing. The second year could cost $1,000 and the additional six months an additional $500 or $600.

I almost always negotiate on behalf of my producer clients with the thought in mind that it is far preferable to pay more money for the second year of the option period than one pays for the first year of the option period. The theory is that after owning the option for a period of one year the producer should be in a pretty good position to know whether or not it will be possible to raise enough money to obtain a director, cast the play, and get it on. If things look good at the end of the year, then the additional larger payment is money well spent, as it is being spent for something that will be used, namely the right to produce the play. Furthermore, the additional payment is, like the first payment, an advance against royalties, and will be deducted from the first royalty payments in all events. If, after owning the option for a year, it seems unlikely that the producer will be able to get this play produced, having paid less for the first year, the money saved can be used for the purchase of another property, one with greater potential.

PLAY COST (ROYALTIES)

The payment previously referred to as an option payment is a payment for the right to produce the play. As soon as the play is presented before paying audiences, the producer makes a weekly payment to the author or owner that is a payment for the presentation of the play. The amount of the payment is directly related to the gross receipts of the producer from the sale of tickets. If the play is a nonmusical, and the author is not well-known or a famous personality, the author is almost always paid 5 percent of the gross weekly box office receipts. If the play is a musical and the author (bookwriter), composer, and lyricist are not famous or even well-known, the royalty payment is almost always 6 percent of the gross weekly box office receipts. The author, composer, and lyricist will either share the 6 percent of the gross weekly box office receipts—with the composer receiving 2 percent, the lyricist receiving 2 percent, and the bookwriter receiving 2 percent; or they will share the 6 percent with the composer and lyricist together receiving 3 percent and the bookwriter receiving 3 percent of the gross weekly box office receipts. The method of sharing is not really the producer's worry or responsibility, except to the extent that the producer must make the payment to specific parties in accordance with the agreement.

If the author (composer, lyricist, or bookwriter, if it is a musical) is well-known, then the royalty payment may be, but need not always be, as much as 10 percent of the gross weekly box office receipts. I have noticed on numerous occasions that some name playwrights have insisted on restricting their royalty payments to an amount that would be paid to a new author, knowing that there are limitations to what an Off-Broadway production can pay for a play and that it is healthy for the play if the royalty payments are not excessive.

When we speak of the gross weekly box office receipts, it must be understood that these receipts are almost always defined as the gross receipts at the box office from the sale of tickets, less theatre-party commission, discount, and cut-rate sales; all admissions taxes present or to be levied; any union pension and welfare deductions; any subscription fees and Actors' Fund benefits.

It is wise to be aware of a useful method of resolving a royalty disagreement that will be helpful in some instances. It may be suggested that the royalty payments should be increased after the production has recouped its original preproduction and production budget; that is, after the total amount of the investment has been recovered. If there is, for an example, a deadlock with the author insisting upon receiving 6 percent of the gross weekly box office receipts, and the producer being inclined to pay no more than 5 percent of the gross weekly box office receipts, it might be helpful to compromise with an arrangement that provides that the author is to be paid 5 percent of the gross weekly box office receipts until the investors have recouped their original investment, at which time the author's royalty payments will be increased to 6 percent of the gross weekly box office receipts or 6 going to 7 percent. This is typical of one of the many compromises that may be made to help resolve disputes and bring about an agreement that might otherwise be difficult or impossible. The concept of a "royalty pool formula" developed for Broadway productions to assure the investors' return of their investment out of first net profits. A simplified concept that is useful Off-Broadway is to reduce all royalty participants' royalty in half (2½ percent of the gross weekly box office receipts) until the production costs have been recouped, at which time they will be increased (to 7 percent, for example) and further increased (to perhaps 8½ percent) after double recoupment of production costs.

WHAT THE OPTION BUYS

An option agreement must somewhere within it state that in consideration of the producer's payment of a certain amount of money, the producer has the right to produce the play to open in an Off-Broadway theatre on or before a specific date set forth in the option agreement. The option should also include the right to produce the play to open in a middle theatre and to do a developmental production Off-Off-Broadway or in a regional theatre before the Off-Broadway or regional production.

WHAT AN OPTION CONDITIONALLY BUYS

Right to Tour

In addition to the right to produce the play Off-Broadway, the producer, under most circumstances, also ought to acquire the rights to produce the play in other areas, conditioned upon the Off-Broadway production running for a certain length of time. For an example, it is not unusual for the producer to acquire the rights to do a tour of the play in the event that the play opens and runs Off-Broadway for twenty-one performances. Bear in mind that under some circumstances this right may be acquired by running less than twenty-one performances or under other circumstances by running more than twenty-one performances. Also be cognizant of the fact that the number of performances for the purpose of this computation is defined in several ways.

Sometimes the contract provides that the play must run for twenty-one performances, counting from the first paid performance, which would, of course, mean from the first paid preview. Other contracts provide that the show must run for twenty-one performances, counting from opening night. When there is a disagreement on this item, a compromise is sometimes reached that would permit one to count twenty-one paid performances from the first paid preview; however, the number of paid previews would be limited to seven, ten, or at the most, fourteen previews. Otherwise, it would be possible to acquire the rights to do a tour by running twenty-one paid previews and not opening the show. Bear in mind also that this method of computing the number of performances that the production has run will be important to us in our later discussion of subsidiary rights. We will see that a producer may acquire an interest in the subsidiary rights providing that the production runs for a certain number of performances.

The option agreement should, of course, set forth the fact that if the producer wishes to do a tour, either a first-class tour or second-class tour, then the producer must, within a certain period of time—for example, up to ninety days after the close of the play, or within one year of the opening of the play—give notice to the author of his or her intention to do the additional production. The option agreement will further provide that, together with the notice, the producer must make an advance payment against royalties, which advance payment will range between $300 and $750. (Although there is no "usual" payment, $500 is more usual than either $300 or $750.) The option will also provide that the tour must open within a specified time after the notice is received, and it is not unusual to provide that the period be designated as eighteen months after receipt of the notice, within which time the first performance on the tour must commence. As is later pointed out in the discussion of subsidiary rights, some time ago, as a result of *The Fantasticks,* which is now in the twenty-ninth year of it's run, they stopped measuring the period of rights based on the date the show closes. Everyone who knows what he is doing now measures from the date the show opens.

A distinction between a first- and a second-class tour is not easily made, but a "first-class tour" is usually defined as a regular evening bill in a "first-class" theatre in a "first-class" manner with a "first-class" cast and a "first-class" director. We know that a Broadway production is a first-class production, and if the New York company of the show goes on tour it will appear in houses considered as first-class theatres and will be a first-class tour. An unusually successful Broadway show may have two or three first-class tours running at the same time. There may also be a second-class tour of the same play. The author's royalties for a second-class tour of a Broadway and Off-Broadway show may be calculated on a guarantee, or a flat-fee, basis; the author's royalties for a first-class tour are calculated on a percentage of the gross weekly box office receipts.

Certain theatres have established themselves as first-class theatres because of the kind of productions that have appeared in them. For example, the Mechanic in Baltimore; the Fisher in Detroit; the O'Keefe and Royal Alexandra in Toronto; the Colonial, Shubert, and Wilbur in Boston; the Shubert, Forrest, Locust, Erlanger, and Walnut in Philadelphia; the Blackstone, McVickers, Shubert, and Studebaker in Chicago; the Shubert in Cincinnati; the Hartford and Music Center in Los Angeles; the Curran and Geary in San Francisco; the National in Washington, D.C.; the Clowes in Indianapolis; the Music Hall in Kansas City; the Hanna in Cleveland; the American in St. Louis; and the Shubert in New Haven, Connecticut, are some of the first-class theatres throughout the country.

In addition to a second-class tour paying the author's royalties on a guarantee or flat-fee basis, other things tend to identify a second-class tour, such as the length of time that the show is presented for each stop.

Second-class tours are usually one-night stands or split weeks. What is commonly referred to as a "bus and truck tour" is almost always a second-class tour that plays one-night stands and split weeks, as is a university or college tour.

If the producer wishes to do a first-class tour, the option agreement will require that the parties concerned enter into a Dramatists Guild, Inc., Approved Production Contract (APC), within a short period after the producer gives notice that he wishes to produce a tour. All royalty payments to the author will be as provided in the Dramatists Guild, Inc., APC that covers such a tour.

In the event that the tour is a second-class tour of an Off-Broadway play, it is not unusual to provide for a royalty payment of 5 percent of the gross box office receipts, or something between 5 percent and 7½ percent of the flat fee payable to the Off-Broadway producer, or an arbitrarily negotiated amount per performance.

English Production

If the play runs for twenty-one performances, more or less depending upon the negotiations, it is also not unusual for the producer to acquire the rights to do an English production of the play. As with the tour provisions, the option agreement will provide that under such circumstances the producer must—within a certain period of time; that is, up to ninety days of the close of the play or within one year of the opening of the play—give notice to the author as provided in the option agreement of his intention to do the English production. With the notice, the agreement will provide that the producer must make an advance payment against royalties that will range between $250 and $600. Three hundred and fifty, or five hundred, dollars is most usual for this advance payment for the rights to do an English production. It is also most usual to provide that the English production must commence within a period between six months and one year after the receipt of the notice.

The agreement may provide that the royalty payment for a West End London production is as provided in the Dramatists Guild, Inc., Approved Production Contract for such a production.

A West End production in London is comparable to a Broadway production in this country. There is one significant difference, however, which is that a West End London production may be mounted for approximately one-third the amount of money that would be required for the same show if produced on Broadway. If the production is other than in the West End of London, then it is not unusual to provide for a straight 5 percent of the gross weekly box office receipts as a royalty payment.

Right to Move to Broadway

The agreement may also further provide that the producer, in addition to the other rights, has the right to initially open the play on Broadway, or to move the play from an Off-Broadway theatre to a Broadway theatre. The agreement will provide that the producer must, immediately upon the decision to open the play on Broadway or to move the play from an Off-Broadway theatre to a Broadway theatre, enter into a Dramatists Guild, Inc., Approved Production Contract (APC), which contract sets forth all of the terms and conditions of the agreement with the author concerning the Broadway production. The APC is not applicable to an Off-Broadway production.*

Subsidiary Rights

Few subjects in connection with Off-Broadway productions cause as much confusion as the area of subsidiary rights. Many persons in theatre toss the term around knowingly but are not sure just exactly what "subsidiaries" are.

Subsidiary rights are rights that accrue to the producer of the original production of the play. For instance, the right to produce the play in other places and in other media, such as a tour or a movie, is a subsidiary right. Confusion arises when people who speak of "subsidiaries" or "subsidiary rights" are not referring to the rights to *produce* the play in other areas or in other media, but rather are referring to the producer's right to share in the author's receipts from productions of the play in other areas and in other media done by others.

There is no doubt that when a play is produced Off-Broadway, the

---

*For a detailed discussion of the Dramatists Guild, Inc., Approved Production Contract, see my newly revised and updated *Producing Theatre.*

production makes a contribution to the value of the play in other media. The author may receive great revenue from the leasing rights—that is, the rights that are granted to theatre groups throughout the country, both amateur and professional, to perform the play—not to mention the fact that the movie and television value of a property is enhanced by a successful Off-Broadway production.

Bear in mind that the author alone retains the right to deal with the property. The author will make the arrangements for, and will execute, the contract if there is a sale for a movie or television production, or for any other use, and the producing company's interest is only in the sharing of the profits, not in the consummation of the actual sale. There is an exception in the case of the original cast album for a musical production in that the producing company, as well as the author, composer, and lyricist, will negotiate and enter into this agreement. However, the producer's being part of this agreement is not because of any interest in the subsidiary rights, but rather because the original cast album will be made using the original cast of the show, and the original cast is employed by the producer. It is, in effect, more than just a recording of the music, but is considered a recording of the production, or rather a part of the production.

Of course, the author must deal in good faith with the property, which the author would normally do for the author's own sake as well as for the producing company's sake. The author may not make a deal that would sacrifice one of the properties he has written, in order to make a much better deal on another property that he has written, for such an arrangement would constitute an unfair dealing with respect to the first property.

For example, an author may have a play that a movie producer is most anxious to make into a movie, for which the author has been offered $500,000. If the producing company that produced the play has an interest in the subsidiary rights, then the author may not offer the right to do the movie for $300,000 on the condition that the movie producer will at the same time purchase another of his works for $200,000.

One should note that the producer will receive the specified percentage if the rights are disposed of during the time set forth in the contract, even if the payment is actually received after this time.

In an Off-Broadway option agreement, the producer may acquire a percentage interest in the author's receipts from subsidiary rights that is either greater or less than what is provided in the Dramatists Guild,

Inc., APC for a Broadway show. The extremes Off-Broadway are (1), the producer may acquire no interest in the subsidiary rights or (2) the producer may acquire 40 percent (or more than 40 percent) upon the first paid performance. Since the first paid performance could be the first paid preview, it is possible in such an extreme instance to acquire an interest in the subsidiary rights without ever opening the play. This has happened but is a rarity and is not the usual situation by any means.

A refusal to grant any interest in the subsidiary rights comes most often from foreign authors, although they are gradually changing this arbitrary position and are becoming educated to the fact of Off-Broadway life. Even a well-known foreign author may make it very difficult, if not impossible, for his producer to raise the money to produce the show if he doesn't grant the producing company an interest in the subsidiary rights income.

You may perhaps wish to produce a play that has been produced before, either on Broadway, in Europe, or elsewhere, and you may be confronted with an author who says "I can't give you an interest in the subsidiary rights as I've already given away an interest to the producer who previously produced the show." There is a way to approach this problem that is sometimes helpful. Your response must be that the producer who produced the show originally ought to want to give some part of the subsidiary rights to the Off-Broadway production, if the Off-Broadway production runs for a certain length of time. There is a good reason why the original producer would want to do this, in view of the fact that a successful Off-Broadway production would increase the value of the subsidiary rights for all concerned. It may also be helpful to suggest that, under such circumstances, in addition to the original producer parting with a portion of the interest he owns in the subsidiary rights, the author should grant the Off-Broadway producer some part of the author's remaining interest in said subsidiary rights.

If the original production owns a 40 percent interest in the author's receipts from subsidiary rights, and you can convince the original producer to part with 20 percent of the author's receipts—that is, half of the original producer's interest—you should also be able to convince the author to give up another 10 percent, which would mean that the Off-Broadway show could potentially receive 30 percent of the receipts from the author's share of the subsidiary rights. As the original production would receive 20 percent, and the author would still be left with 50 percent, the author in effect is getting two bites of the same apple, and under such circumstances should not complain too much about giving up an additional 10 percent interest. At the same time, the original producer will discover that the interest in the subsidiary rights is essentially "found" money, and will probably not complain too much about having given up some percentage. The Off-Broadway production will also receive something slightly less, but this is the compromise that one has to make if one wants to produce a show that has already been produced.

The Off-Broadway option must make provision for the period of time within which the sale must be made for the producer to share in the profits from the subsidiary rights, and must make provision for the amount of the profits that the producer will receive. In the case of the length of time, the extremes would be (1) two years and (2) the life of the copyright. What has become most usual is that the interest of the Off-Broadway producer will be paid if any rights are disposed of during a period of either seven years, ten years, or fifteen years after the official opening of the play. Perhaps the most commonly used period is ten years for a dramatic play and either ten or twelve years for a musical play, and was for a period of time measured from the close of the Off-Broadway play. I made such a provision in the contract to produce *The Fantasticks,* which is now in its twenty-ninth year and still going strong. When *The Fantasticks* was well into its run, agents and attorneys representing authors decided it would be wiser to measure this period from the opening of the show rather than from the closing.

Between the extreme of no interest in the subsidiary rights and the extreme of granting a 40 percent (or larger) interest to the producer upon the first paid performance is the area where most contract negotiations end up. In an attempt to express the concept that the value that an Off-Broadway production contributes to the property is directly proportionate to the length of time that the play runs Off-Broadway, there has developed the idea of graduating the producer's share of the author's receipts so that the longer the play runs, the more the Off-Broadway producer receives from subsidiary rights. The producer's share is generally graduated between 10 percent and 40 percent of the receipts. It is not unusual to grant the Off-Broadway production 10 percent of the author's receipts if the play runs for twenty-one performances; 20 percent if the play runs for forty-two performances; 30 percent if the play runs for fifty-five performances; and 40 percent if the play runs for over sixty-five performances. This is the measure that I almost always use whether I represent an author or a producer or both.

I think it is a fair and reasonable measure and would not discourage investors.

The option agreement must explicitly set forth the time that one starts counting the number of performances, whether from the first paid preview, from opening night, or from the first paid preview with a limitation on the number of previews that are counted.

Author's representatives will endeavor to sell you on the idea that you should accept 10 percent of the author's receipts if the play runs for twenty-one performances from opening night; 20 percent if the play runs for fifty-six performances from the opening night; 30 percent if the play runs for seventy-five performances from opening night; and 40 percent if the play runs for ninety-nine performances or over, counting from opening night. On the other hand, the producer's attorney will try to sell the author's representative on the idea that the producer should receive percentages based on fewer numbers of performances: 10 percent of the author's share if the play runs for twenty-one paid performances; 20 percent if the play runs for thirty-five paid performances; should receive 30 percent if the play runs for forty-eight paid performances; and should receive 40 percent if the play runs for fifty-six performances or more, counting from the first paid performance.

Of course, it goes without saying that whether one counts from the first paid preview or from opening night, whether the interest of the Off-Broadway producer in the subsidiary rights extends over a period of three years from the opening of the Off-Broadway production or fifty-six years from the opening of the Off-Broadway production, and the extent of the producer's interest in the rights will depend upon the relative bargaining power of each of the parties.

BILLING CREDITS

Another important provision in all option agreements is the provision concerning billing credits for the author. It is an especially important provision in the Off-Broadway agreement since it very often provides the most meaningful consideration that the author receives. I have often said, partly in jest, that in negotiating an option agreement, the real quarrels do not concern money but rather the size of the type and whose name comes first. It's mostly only a matter of ego in a business where the amount of money one receives and one's importance in the profession is measured by the number of times that one's name is seen as well as the size of one's name. In a sense, the argument about billing credit is an argument about money. Some stories concerning billing credit border upon the absurd; however, in the Off-Broadway arena, where the authors are paid relatively little, the authors' right to make their names known must be considered extremely important.

Some contracts provide that the author's name must appear in paid advertising, houseboards, billboards, and programs. Teaser ads and alphabetical listing ads, commonly known as ABC ads, are usually the exception where the name need not appear. Resist the author's attempt to have his or her name appear wherever the name of the play appears, as there is no room on most marquees for an author's name.

Sometimes there is a provision that the author's name will be a certain size in relation to the size of the type used for the title of the play; sometimes it is provided that the author's name will be at least one-half the size of type used for the title of the play; or one-quarter of the size of type used for the title of the play. Sometimes an author insists on a provision that his or her name will be as large or larger than any other name that appears in the advertisement, program, or whatever. This may be a self-defeating provision, for the producer may then be prevented from signing a particular star or a prominent director because of the kind of billing that star, or prominent director, insists upon in order to do the play. If a star is adamant that his name be larger than any other name, then it may very well be in the author's best interest to let the star have his way. A producer must have the leeway to function so that the best artistic performers may be engaged for the play.

If there is more than one author, it is most usual that the authors' names appear in alphabetical order, unless one of the authors is much better known and thus may insist on being first under all circumstances. Many name writers know that the prominent use of their name by the producer will mean ticket sales for the producer. Ironically enough, those who are in the best position to insist upon the most desirable billing credits often insist on nothing, confident that they will receive the most desirable billing credits because it is in the interest of the producer to do this.

Billing Box

Through the years, to alleviate the billing credit problem, especially if the producer wanted to use the title in a logo that is huge on the poster, the concept of a "billing box" has developed. This gives the producer the right to have a small box with all credits measured by the size of the title in the box, or by some other name in the box, and not measured by the huge title which is part of the logo on the rest of the poster. Billing boxes are in common use. Look for them the next time you see some play posters.

HOUSE SEATS

An option agreement will almost always contain provisions providing that the author may purchase a certain number of house seats. House seats are prime seats that are reserved for purchase by various persons associated with the production and are usually held by the theatre for the party until 6 P.M. of the day before each evening performance and until 12 noon of the day before each matinee performance. If the tickets are not purchased by then by the house seat owner, they are sold to the general public. It is usual for a producer to reserve one or two pairs of house seats for purchase by the author (more or less depending upon the size of the theatre) and five or six pairs for opening night.

AUTHORS' APPROVALS

An option agreement will provide that the author shall have director approval, cast approval, and sometimes stage manager, costume designer, and set designer approval. In the case of a musical, the composer may have musical director and choreographer approval. It should always further provide that the approvals will not be unreasonably withheld, and that if the author does not approve or disapprove within a certain specified time—that is, within three to seven days after the request for approval—that the failure to respond will be considered an approval. The author may be out of the country or otherwise inaccessible, and the play must never suffer as a result of any one person's unavailability or disinterest.

It goes without saying that the agreement should provide that no changes will be made in the script without the author's approval. Rest assured that the author or the author's representative will make certain that this provision is part of the agreement. The producer may also request that this approval by the author will also not be unreasonably withheld, but usually will not get it.

ARBITRATION

Options very often contain an arbitration clause, which provides that if there is a dispute, instead of going to court to settle it, the parties consent that it may be settled by an impartial arbitrator, usually in accordance with the rules of the American Arbitration Association. The advantages of an arbitration are that it is informal, speedy, less expensive, and there is a clear probability that the dispute will be settled by a person or persons who know the business. Since the parties have an opportunity to select the arbitrators, the selection should be from a group of individuals involved in show business so that the party making the determination will have the background necessary to properly decide the issues.

ASSIGNABILITY OF OPTION

The producer is given the right to assign the option agreement; however, this is usually granted with some limitations. An assignment is in effect a transfer. If one assigns a contract, the person taking the assignment—that is, the person acquiring the rights to the contract—will receive all of the benefits of the contract, but at the same time assumes all of the contract obligations. The agreement may limit the assignment to only a limited partnership or corporation or other entity in which the producer is one of the major principals. The author originally makes his agreement with a specific producer and does not want someone else producing the play, thus the provision that the entity must have as one of the principals the producer to whom the grant was originally made. An assignment is made subject to the terms and conditions of the original option agreement, which means that the producing company to which the producer makes the assignment must be bound by the agreement. It is often provided that even if there is an assignment, the original producer will continue to remain responsible for the obligations of the contract.

OPTION OF FIRST REFUSAL

The option may also contain a provision that the producer, if he successfully produces the play, may have an option of first refusal on future plays of the author. This means simply that the producer may match any other bona fide offer for the play during a fixed period of time and obtain the rights to produce the play under the same terms and conditions as the bona fide offer. An "option of first refusal" is a common term used in the business and it means, namely, that the person holding the option during this given time must first be given an opportunity to make the purchase, or do whatever is required, before a sale may be made to someone else. There is much criticism of this kind of a provision since, it is argued—and with good reason, that if the producer produces the play and he gets along well with the author, there is every reason in the world for the author to make certain that this producer produces his next play. However, if they do not get along, the producer should not produce the next play no matter what the contractual arrangements may be.

BUYER'S MARKET

In the option negotiations it is well to bear in mind that Off-Broadway is a buyer's market, in that an author who has never had a play produced often needs an Off-Broadway production as a stepping stone to other writing assignments. There is this to be said, however, that I do not, in all my experience, know of a really good play that has not been produced. I do know of really good plays that have been badly produced. However, if one has authored a play that has commercial and artistic possibilities, there is every reason to believe that this play will eventually be produced, "buyers' market" or not.

For an example of a typical option agreement that might be applicable to an Off-Broadway play see Appendix A. Please bear in mind that this is not an "average" agreement, as there is no such thing as an average agreement.

ADAPTATIONS

No one in his right mind would go into the street, find an automobile that appeals to him, and start washing and polishing that automobile in the hope that, when the owner returned to the car, he could purchase the automobile from him. Although no one would do this to an automobile, some people very often, without thinking, do obtain a property that belongs to someone else, and go to great lengths to improve the property without first owning it. What I am referring to is the frequent practice of adapting a novel, a movie, or a nonmusical as a musical for a stage production when the basic rights are not owned. Composers do it, writers do it, even producers do it. When one wishes to adapt, or cause to be adapted, a novel, story, movie, or whatever that was written by someone else, one must first acquire the rights to make the adaptation.

Merger of Rights

The agreement with the owner of the basic work and the adaptors should provide that if the play opens and runs for a specified period of time all dramatic rights (grand performing rights as distinguished from the small performing rights) in the basic work merge with the adaptation and become one entity and can only be dealt with as one work. If the play does not run for the period of time specified, then each contributor owns his or her respective contribution and can dispose of it any way he or she pleases.

Grand rights are those needed to perform the music in a dramatic fashion, while only small performing rights are required for nondramatic performances. If there exists a story connecting the songs together, the performance is considered a musical play and dramatic, thus requiring grand rights. If there is no story but just improvised patter connecting the songs, the performance may be more like a non-dramatic nightclub act, requiring only small rights. But the kind of dialogue between songs is not the only basis on which to decide if a storyline exists. Sets, costumes, and props could, with the music and lyrics, create a dramatic sequence conveying a story, especially if one or all of those elements are similar to the sets, costumes, and props used in a play from which the songs were originally performed. Thus, although television, radio, nightclub, and concert performances of songs usually require only small performing rights, if a story is conveyed through any of the elements of dialogue, sets, costumes, and props, grand rights may be required. There are no definite rules that apply in order to determine whether a story is being told or not.

Basic Work—Copyright Ownership

It is sometimes difficult to determine who is the owner of the "basic work" (as it is referred to), and the first thing that must be done is to obtain a copyright search. The copyright search should disclose whether or not the basic work is in the public domain, and if it is not in the public domain, who the copyright owner of record is. When we speak about "public domain," we of course mean that the work does not enjoy copyright protection, either because the copyright has expired, the work was published without filing with the copyright office or some other reason. The copyright laws were recently changed so that the copyright on a work exists for the life of the author plus fifty years. When one sells a copyright—that is, assigns the copyright to someone else—a document should be recorded in the copyright office. The copyright search will disclose this document if it has been filed.

Royalties for Basic Work

The negotiations then commence with the copyright owner to obtain the rights to do the adaptation. It is most usual to pay from 1 to 2 percent of the gross weekly box office receipts to the owner of the basic work. Furthermore, the owner of the basic work will want an interest in the subsidiaries and will request, and will usually get, that proportionate part of any payment that his or her royalty bears to the aggregate royalties payable to all of the authors (including the payment to the owner of the basic work). This means that if a total of 9 percent is paid to all the authors (including the payment to the owner of the basic work), and the owner of the basic work is paid a royalty of 1 percent, then the owner of the basic work will share in the subsidiaries by receiving one-ninth of the author's share of said subsidiaries.

Basic Work Option Fee (Adaptations)

It is not unusual for a producer to find a basic work that he wants adapted, and to cause the adaptation to be made. In addition to the provision for royalty payments, there are many other details of the agreement dealing with the acquisition of the rights to do an adaptation of the basic work. For an Off-Broadway production, it is not unusual to obtain these rights without the payment of a large sum of money as a fee or as an advance against royalty payments. In some instances, it is possible to obtain these rights without any advance payment, although it is not unusual to pay the sum of $500 or $1,000 as an advance against royalty payments. This payment will purchase the right to do the adaptation, which must be completed within a specified time, often within one year, and the right to produce the play within a specified time, usually a year after the completion of the adaptation.

The Adaptor

An Off-Broadway producer will have to find a bookwriter (and in the case of a musical, a composer and lyricist) to do the adaptation. Most writers would not begin to do a play for a producer for a Broadway production without a payment of money, the amount of money being dependent upon the reputation of the writer—and how badly the writer wants to do the play. Off-Broadway, it is not unusual to find writers who are willing to do an adaptation on "spec," which means that the work is done on the speculation that, after it is completed, it will be sold. A full option agreement must be entered into with the person doing the adaptation, which agreement will provide that the producer may produce the play after it is completed. It usually further provides that the producer shall continue to own the basic rights, and if the producer is not happy with the adaptation, the rights in the basic work revert to the producer, who can at this point go out and hire another writer to do the adaptation of the work.

The important lesson to learn is that, before we improve something, we should make certain that we own it, whether it is an automobile, a house, a novel, or a movie.

CHAPTER 2

Co-Production Agreements

EITHER BEFORE OR AFTER you've optioned the property, you may decide that you wish to produce the play together with someone else. If this is the case, it is wise for you to have an agreement in the nature of a co-production agreement, which sets forth your duties and obligations to each other. Before the limited partnership or other entity that will produce the play comes into existence, you and your co-producer are operating as an entity, usually in the nature of a "joint venture." A joint venture is a kind of partnership, and the one most important fact to bear in mind is that, like other partnerships, you are responsible for all the actions of your "joint venturer" in connection with the business of the joint venture.

Although the agreement between you may state that you will each be equally responsible for any expenditures or any losses, as far as creditors of the joint venture are concerned, each of you is responsible for the total amount of the commitment. That is, if one of two joint venturers (partners) obligates the joint venture (partnership) to the extent of $4,000 for advertising, or for any other business expenditure, each of the two partners, as between themselves, may be responsible for $2,000 of this obligation. The creditor, however, may look to either one for his $4,000 and if one of the partners does not have any money, the creditor may collect the whole $4,000 from the solvent member of the joint venture.

The co-production agreement will state that the co-producers own a property they wish to produce, that they are going to endeavor to raise the money for the production, and when the money is raised, they will be the general partners of a limited partnership that will be formed. This agreement will set forth the basic terms that will be incorporated into the limited partnership agreement. There will also be set forth the amount of the budget, the method of sharing profits and losses by each of the partners, whether or not the partners' profits are related to the amount of money that each producer raises, how the producers' fees are to be shared, how the cash office charge is shared, and so forth.

The co-producers may agree that they will share equally in the profits of the company irrespective of which partner is responsible for the raising of most of the money for the show. On the other hand, sometimes co-producers wish to relate the share of the profits more directly to the amount of money that each one raises. If one is going to relate the sharing of the profits to the amount of money that each co-producer raises, one ought also to relate the other important contributions to the production made by each partner to the sharing of the profits. For an example, the partner who discovered the property could claim a larger percentage of the profits for this contribution, the party influencing the star could claim something extra for that, and so on.

The next logical step is an attempt to balance all of the items that each of the co-producers contributes, and to relate the share of the profits to the relative importance of each contribution. So very often, when co-producers sit down and try to balance the contribution that each one makes to a production, they discover that the importance of each contribution is difficult to measure. As a result, they end up deciding to share equally in the profits and losses, with all parties agreeing to contribute their best efforts to the production in all ways.

FRONT MONEY

Where the "front money" is coming from, and what will be given for the front money is another item that must be dealt with in the co-production agreement. Front money is money that is obtained for the purpose of paying all the expenses that occur prior to the money-raising for the production itself, and prior to the receipt of the total capitalization and release of the other investors' funds.

The regulations pursuant to the Arts and Cultural Affairs Laws of the State of New York define *front money,* stating that it may be used only for the following preproduction expenses of a proposed production: "fees; advances; deposits or bonds made for the purpose of purchasing options on a book, play, or other underlying materials; engaging creative personnel; securing a theatre; retaining legal, accounting, and other professional advisors; preparing offering documents; the costs of a workshop to be presented by the issuer or any other purpose reasonably related to the production for which the front money was raised." The front money that the producer may raise, if he doesn't use his own money, is given on the condition that the producer assign a certain percentage interest of the producer's partnership profits to the person who puts up the front money.

Front money is discussed here because it is often the reason for taking on a co-producer. Sometimes the co-producer will contribute the front money in exchange for your contributing the property, or at least for your discovery of the property. Even if both co-producers are to equally furnish front money, the facts, in all events, must be set forth in the co-production agreement.

The co-production agreement will also set forth how decisions are to be made and what happens if there is a deadlock, as it is very important that there be some quick resolution in the event that there is a disagreement. In the case of an artistic decision, two co-producers may provide that, in the event of a dispute between them, the director will make the final determination. They may also provide that in the event of a business dispute, the question will be settled by the attorney, the accountant, or anyone else whose business judgment both producers would respect. Other possibilities exist for settling such disputes as various as one's imagination.

The agreement should also set forth who may sign checks and who may sign other obligations of the joint venture. The ever-prevailing question of credits must be dealt with in this agreement; that is, whose name comes first. It is usual to provide that wherever the name of one co-producer appears, the name of all co-producers will appear in type of the same size, prominence, and boldness. Billing credits are usually in alphabetical order in the absence of other more pressing considerations. An arbitration clause may be included, which, as we know, means that in the event of a dispute, rather than going to court, an impartial person would make the determination.

The co-production agreement should also set forth the personnel that the producers have agreed upon who will be employed by the show; namely, the attorney, the accountant, and the general manager, as well as any other personnel that there is agreement upon at this stage.

The joint venture will cease upon the organization of the limited partnership unless the parties abandon the play and decide to terminate it sooner.

A sample of a typical Co-Production Agreement can be found in Appendix B. Again the caution that this is not an "average" agreement, as there is no such thing Off-Broadway.

ASSOCIATE PRODUCER—MONEY

We have previously discussed a co-production agreement in the nature of a joint venture, and something should be said at this point about arrangements with associate producers. A co-producer, in a sense, is a partner who may have an equal amount of control in the running of the business, both artistically and from a business point of view. More realistically, an associate producer usually spells one thing and that is "money." Most associate producers get such billing credit for having furnished, usually through someone else's investment, a certain amount of money for the show. What else the associate producer gets, in addition to associate producer billing, depends upon how badly the producer needs the amount of money that the associate producer can furnish. A part of the producer's profits, yes, but it cannot include any decision-making on the artistic or business level. If the associate producer is involved in any of the business decisions of the partnership, he may be exposing himself to the liability of a general partner. A smart producer, however, will take into consideration any suggestions made by an associate producer even though there is no obligation to accept the associate's advice.

It is usual for the producer to give an associate producer 1 percent of the profits of the producing company payable from the general partners' share for each 3, 4, or 5 percent of the producing company purchased by an investment for which the associate producer is responsible. This must not be confused with front money. Front money, which we previously discussed, is money that can be used prior to the capitalization and formation of the producing company for the specific reasons set forth above. Front money is risk capital in that if the show is not produced, then the front money investor loses the money spent on the production. The person furnishing the front money will generally get 1 percent of the profits of the producing company, payable from the general partners' share for each 1 percent of the producing company that that particular amount of money would buy from the limited partners' share of the profits. It is not unusual to give a person who furnishes front money an associate producer's billing credits as well as the percentage interest in the show. The agreement with associate producers must always give consideration to the order of the names in the billing credits and the size, prominence, and boldness of the billing credit type.

CHAPTER 3

The Producing Company

AFTER HAVING ACQUIRED THE PROPERTY, you must give consideration to the type of entity that will produce the play. When we talk about an "entity," we mean the producing company. Of course, you may produce the play yourself in your own name instead of using a different, separate entity, but then you will be the sole producer and must furnish all of the money. If you borrowed all the money or planned to use your own money, you might do it in this fashion; however, a play is almost always financed by persons making investments in a producing company rather than making a loan to the producer or a producer furnishing all of the money himself. If investors are going to give you money, some agreement must be reached between you as the producer and your investors. The entity that will produce the play will either be a partnership or a corporation. Usually, it is a partnership—a special kind of partnership—known as a "limited partnership."

PARTNERSHIP OR CORPORATION

Limited Liability

Why use a limited partnership to produce the play—why not a corporation? This is a very good question. We rule out a general partnership, or a joint venture, immediately because it does not give the investors the benefit of limited liability. Limited liability means simply that the investors, the limited partners, are only obligated to the extent of their investment (or in some instances, if there is an overcall provided for in the agreement, they are liable to the extent of an additional 10, 15, or 20 percent. The general partner, the producer in a limited partnership, runs the business and is personally responsible for all of the obligations of the partnership. If the production goes over budget and more money is spent than is raised, this becomes the obligation of the general partner. This is not the obligation of the limited partners, assuming, of course, that the limited partnership is properly organized in strict accordance with the terms of the partnership laws of the State of New York.

We could also give our investors limited liability if we formed a corporation and made them corporate stockholders. In this fashion, the producers could be the officers and directors and the investors would not be liable beyond the original investment.

Tax Benefits

Although corporate stockholders enjoy limited liability in the same sense that limited partners do, there are certain tax advantages that the investors may enjoy with a partnership that they would not have with a corporation. If the company loses money—that is, if the venture does not make enough money to return to the investors their total investment—the loss for income tax purposes is considered an ordinary loss, which may be offset against ordinary income if a partnership is the producer. Each partner would consider his or her investment to the extent it is lost as an ordinary loss.

Recent changes in the Tax Code limit the deductibility of losses arising from limited partnership interests ("passive activity losses") to the extent of gains from passive activities. The limits on deductibility will be phased in gradually until 1990. The deductibility of losses are deferred until the limited partner disposes of his entire interest in the partnership.

If a corporation is the producing company and it loses money, the loss is in the nature of a capital loss. Each investor may offset the loss, first against capital gains, and the balance, if any, may then be offset up to $3,000 of ordinary income. Since most investors need a loss that can be offset against income more than they need a capital loss, the benefit to the investor of a partnership is considerable in this respect.

The other important consideration is that partnership income is taxed but once. If the producing company is a corporation and makes a profit, the corporation first pays income tax on the income and then when the profits are distributed to the investors as dividends, the investors again pay an income tax on the dividends.

CORPORATION AS A PARTNER

The laws of the State of New York were changed effective September 1, 1963, to provide that a corporation may be a general partner or limited partner. You may ask why not combine the advantages of a corporation and the advantages of a partnership. That is, the producer or producers first organize a corporation and make this corporation the general partner of the limited partnership, so that the investors may have the tax benefits of a partnership, and the producer as well as the investors may have the advantage of limited liability. There are some instances where this may be advisable. If the corporation is substantial and has large assets, then there may be good reason and less risk to do this. The Internal Revenue Service has taken the position that unless the corporate general partner has assets in an amount equal to a certain percentage of the total budget for the show (the percentage amount is a variable amount), then the limited partnership will be taxed as a corporation.

There is still another alternative if one wishes a corporation to be a general partner and if one of the producers is less affluent than the other. One might include the less-affluent individual who is not worried about personal liability with the corporation as the general partner of the limited partnership. In this event, if all of the other Internal Revenue requirements were complied with, there would be no question but that the partnership would be taxed as a partnership rather than a corporation, no matter how rich or insolvent the individual general partner is, so long as there is an individual in addition to the corporation as one of the general partners. The problem is that the less-affluent partner would most often feel put upon to be the responsible general partner, being the one least able to take the financial loss. For this reason, the parties usually end up as individual general partners, rather than corporate general partners, unless, of course, the corporation happens to be very rich.

THE LIMITED PARTNERSHIP

How and What Is Limited

What is a theatrical limited partnership agreement? What is a partnership agreement? What is limited about this agreement? The partnership agreement is an agreement between the general partner (the producer) and the limited partners (the investors), which agreement sets forth their duties and obligations with respect to each other concerning the production of the play and their respective rights in the play and the proceeds from the play. The word "limited," as we have previously noted, refers to something that should be limited, namely the investors' liability, and if the agreement is properly drafted and the law complied with, it will, in fact, be limited to the extent of the investment (plus the possible overcall if provided for) and no more. An investor who is a limited partner need not be concerned that he or she will be personally responsible if the producer goes over budget and spends more money than he has raised.

In a partnership other than a limited partnership—that is, in a general partnership—each partner is responsible to the creditors for all of the partnership obligations. In a limited partnership agreement, this kind of obligation is assumed solely by the general partner. One of the things that distinguishes the general partner from the limited partners is that the general partner's liability is unlimited.

In exchange for the limitation of liability of the investors, you, as the producer, are given the right to be the "chief" and solely in charge of all the decisions of the partnership. The general partner has the say in all respects, and as the producer, you are in a position to make all of the business and artistic decisions without any interference from the limited partners. As producer, if you want to listen to a limited partner's advice, you may do so, or you may ignore such advice and do as you please.

Legal Publication (Theatrical Exception)

In order to insure that the liability of the investors is limited, the law must be strictly complied with. The law of the State of New York provides that a Certificate of Limited Partnership must be filed in the County Clerk's office of the county in which the principal office of the partnership is located. The Partnership Law of the State of New York also provides that the contents of a Certificate of Limited Partnership, or digest thereof, must be published once a week for six consecutive weeks in two newspapers in the county where the certificate is filed. There is one exception to this rule that is part of the Arts and Cultural Affairs Law, which provides that the publication is not necessary for a limited partnership for a stage production (not a film or television production) if part of the name of the partnership contains the words *Limited Partnership.* Thus, production partnerships are not called the "Hooray Company" anymore but rather the "Hooray Limited Partnership."

I have had occasion to examine a certain widely used joint venture agreement that purported to protect the investors but that, in fact, did not accomplish this purpose. The investors may never have had to reach into their pockets for additional money because the general partner did not go over budget, or if he did, he personally paid the difference, but there is no good reason why a limited partner should even be exposed to the possibility of being hurt in that fashion. When he parts with his money, if the investor buys nothing else he should at least get a limitation of his liability to the amount of money which he actually invests and no more.

It is extremely important that you be aware there are only two ways that an investor's liability may be limited and both are creatures of statute: (1) a limited partnership, and (2) a corporation.

If persons are doing business together in any way and they have not gone through the proper legal procedure to organize a limited partnership or a corporation, then, as far as creditors of the business are concerned, they are general partners, no matter what they may agree between themselves. There is nothing else that they can be but general partners of a partnership, even if they give it some other label.

LIMITED PARTNERSHIP AGREEMENT FORM

There is no standard form of theatrical partnership agreement. There is a form that was in common use by many attorneys thirty years ago, a form originally intended for Broadway productions. Even for a Broadway show, this particular form must be adapted by adding particular provisions at the end that are especially applicable to the particular show. For an Off-Broadway production, this form is sometimes adapted to the situation; however, it is usually necessary to make so many additions and changes in this form that it is deemed inadvisable to use it under any circumstances.

Profit Sharing

Almost all limited partnership agreements used in theatre have some things in common. One common thing is that almost all provide that the investors in the show will receive 50 percent of the profits of the producing company, which includes not only the profits earned at the box office, but also the profits earned by the company from all sources, including the profits from subsidiaries. They are rare, but there are some producers who will give the limited partners 60 percent of the profits and retain only 40 percent for themselves. On the other hand, there are producers who, under certain circumstances, limit the investors' share of the profits to 50 percent of the profits from only the gross box office receipts, and they do not give the investors any share in the subsidiary rights, or give only a limited interest in some of the subsidiary rights. This is a more common practice if the producer is producing a play by a universally well-known author or composer, when the producer knows there will be many persons clamoring to invest in the production. The producer may know that there will be no problem selling the investors' shares without giving away an interest in the subsidiary rights. However, this is most assuredly an Off-Broadway rarity. It does happen sometimes on Broadway but there have been few occasions when it has happened Off-Broadway.

Budget and Capitalization

The limited partnership agreement will provide that the general partner has acquired the right to produce the play and will assign all of the rights to the limited partnership when it is formed. The general partner will receive the money as it is invested and must hold it in a trust account until enough money is raised, as set forth in the agreement, to produce the play. If the partnership agreement is signed in a certain way, an investor may give the producer the right to use his or her money before the total budget is raised.

If any investor authorizes the use of his or her money before the total budget is raised (whether or not it is front money, as previously discussed), it is important that the producer's attorney file the Certificate of Limited Partnership before the funds are actually used by the general partner. The partnership is not formed until the certificate is filed, and, until it is formed, the investor does not have the intended limited liability. Use of investors' funds prior to the proper formation of the limited partnership would expose them to the liability of a general partner. The certificate can always be amended at a later date—when the total budget is raised to include those later investing or before full capitalization if any investors authorize the use of their funds prior to capitalization. If you know that you can produce the play on $200,000, with a small reserve, but that it would be much preferable to do it with $250,000 and a larger reserve, you should provide in the limited partnership agreement that the budget is $250,000 but that you can produce the play for $200,000 or something between $200,000 and $250,000. You may be faced with the alternative of doing the play either with $200,000 or something between $200,000 and $250,000, or not doing the show at all.

If you do finally capitalize for less than the larger amount than you originally sold the shares for, then instead of returning money to the investors, each limited partner will end up with an additional percentage of the show for his investment. That is, a limited partner would invest $5,000 for a 1 percent interest in the profits of a $250,000 show or would invest $4,000 for a 1 percent interest in the profits of a $200,000 show. The producer originally starts selling 1 percent of the profits for $5,000. If he later decides to capitalize the show for $200,000, then the $5,000 investment would purchase 1.25 percent of the net profits of the production and the investor would receive this share. An investor is investing a fixed dollar mount. In such a case an investor may get more than 1 percent for a $5,000 investment but may not get less than 1 percent for the $5,000.

Bear in mind that the Rules and Regulations of the Attorney General of the State of New York, promulgated under the Arts and Cultural Affairs Law, will not permit a difference of more than 25 percent between the smaller budgeted amount and the larger budgeted amount; that is, the smaller amount may not be more than 25 percent smaller than the larger budget.

The reserve is a necessary part of every budget because it is most rare that a show will do sold-out business immediately after it opens. Even with rave reviews, it sometimes takes three to four weeks or more for the word of mouth to catch on and for the tickets to start disappearing from the racks. However, a producer faced with the possibility of doing the show with a smaller reserve, or not doing the show at all, may wisely choose the former alternative.

Abandonment

Of course, the limited partnership agreement will provide that the producer may abandon the production at any time. This is a necessary requirement, as it is sometimes essential to abandon the production before opening night. In the event of abandonment, the only obligation to the investors is the return of all monies on hand and an accounting for the other monies spent on the production.

Payment of Profits

The agreement will provide that the profits will be paid to the investors monthly, after payment of all debts, and after establishment and maintenance of a cash reserve in a given amount. The excess, if any, is then paid to the limited partners until they have recouped their original investment. With an Off-Broadway show, the cash reserve can vary between $20,000 and $50,000. The maintenance of a cash reserve is important to get through some of those bad weeks that can sneak in when least expected and also when very much expected. The agreement will also provide that the limited partners may examine the books of account of the partnership, and that the general partner will furnish accounting statements as required by law.

Return of Profits to Company

The agreement will also provide that if monies have been paid to the limited partners during the run of the show and money is needed, then the general partner may request that the limited partners return first the profits and then the capital (the original investment) that was returned to them, up to the total amount that they had initially invested in the show. One can understand that it is possible for a production to do good business for six or eight months—such good business that some of the money is returned to the investors—and then hit a slow, slack season when the production, having used up the reserve, to stay alive, really needs the money it previously paid out to the partners. Under such circumstances, the money paid to the investors would have to be returned by them if requested by the producer. Of course, it goes without saying that to the extent that the limited partners return any profits paid to them, the general partner must also return a proportionate share of the profits that have been paid to him.

Producer's Fee and Cash Office Charge

In addition to the share of the profits to which the producer is entitled, the producer will also receive a producer's fee and a "cash office charge." The cash office charge reimburses the producer for the expenditures by him in maintaining an office (which includes stationery, rent, secretary, etc.) for the play.

The producer need not have a separate office and may use his own apartment and still collect the cash office charge. It is not uncommon for a producer to install a second telephone line in his apartment and use the apartment as the office of the producing company. The producer also need not use the office exclusively for the production. For that matter, the producer need not work solely and exclusively on the production, but may at the same time produce more than one show or be engaged in another business.

The producer's fee for an Off-Broadway show is usually most nominal. It should be a weekly fee of 1 or 2 percent of the gross weekly box office receipts, or it may be 1 percent going to 1½ percent or 2 percent after recoupment of the total production costs. Sometimes it is a fixed flat fee between $250 and $350. The cash office charge, which usually starts two weeks before rehearsals and ends two weeks after the close of the show, will most usually be between $150 and $400 per week.

The amount of the producer's fee and the amount of the cash office charge are most usually related to the amount of the total budget of the show. A show budgeted at $150,000 would in all probability make a payment to the producer, as his fee, an amount that is far less than the payment to the producer for a show budgeted for $300,000. The cash office charge would likewise be a variable depending upon the amount of the total budget.

Bonds and Bond Deals

A limited partnership agreement will probably provide that under certain circumstances the limited partners may, in lieu of investing money, deposit a bond with Actors' Equity Association (AEA) or other unions. There may also be a provision for the deposit of a bond by a limited partner or other person under the circumstances that the person who puts up the bond money will get his or her money back prior to any money being paid to the limited partners. It is usually provided that such an arrangement will not reduce the amount of the limited partners' interest in the profits. Thus a person putting up bond money under such circumstances may receive a share of the limited partners' profits in exchange for the bond, but must be further compensated either from the general partner's share of the profits or in some other fashion by the general partner.

Actually, most productions are budgeted so that the bond money need not be used; thus, if the agreement provides that the bond money is to be returned to the party who furnished it, it can readily be seen that the party making such an investment has much less risk than the other limited partners. The entire capitalization may be spent and the bond may remain intact to be returned in full to the bond dealer. When I say that the partnership agreement usually provides that the investor who puts up bond money may not reduce the share of the limited partners' investment by so doing, I am stating what is the usual case. Of course, the limited partnership agreement may provide otherwise. So long as it's not contrary to public policy and all of the limited partners agree to it, it's possible to provide anything in the agreement. To my way of thinking, it would be most unfair to treat limited partners differently. Thus, to arrange that one limited partner would get his money back before the other limited partners get theirs simply because his money was used for the bond is in my opinion unfair.

What bonds are we talking about? The Actors' Equity Association bond is in the amount of two weeks' salary, plus two weeks' pension and welfare for each Equity performer., and a $100 bookkeeping charge. The Association of Theatrical Press Agents and Managers (ATPAM) bond is two weeks' salary, plus vacation, pensions, and welfare payments, and for the press agent only a $500 expense-account bond. In the event that the bond is not used to pay salaries, then the entire bond, including the bookkeeping charge, is returned to the producing company.

If you are producing a musical, the American Federation of Musicians Local 802 will insist upon a bond in the amount of one week's salary, plus vacation, pension, and welfare payments for each musician. If the producer is not a member of the League of Off-Broadway Producers, he must post a bond with the Society of Stage Directors and Choreographers for the full fee and advance payable to the director and to the choreographer, if there is one.

The theatre's advance deposit is in the nature of a bond; however, it is usually nonreturnable in that the amount on deposit is used to pay for the License Agreement. The theatre will expect a four weeks' advance deposit, usually, and may expect between $500 and $7,500 to cover any unpaid bills or damages to the theatre. The advance deposit to the theatre is almost always applied against the fees for the first week and the last three weeks.

Beware of the fact that there are operating in the theatrical area bond dealers who are eager to make the bond investment for almost any show, on the most onerous terms. If a production is so nearly capitalized that all that is needed is another $25,000 or $30,000 and that last amount is getting difficult to obtain, it seems at first blush like a very prudent thing to have someone come in and furnish the bond money. The problem is that most of these people who are willing to furnish bond money don't want to take the risk that is inherent in theatrical investing; they want an edge, an advantage over everyone else who is making an investment, plus the fact that they expect to get a greater remuneration than the other investors. This happens because the bond wheeler-dealers know how desperate a producer may be to get the last few dollars, the final money to complete the capitalization of the show, and they take advantage of this fact. Be cautious of any bond deal. Know that when you start out to raise your money, you will need enough money to cover the bonds. When someone approaches you to make it easier for you to get your bond money, make certain you don't part with more than you should in exchange for a quick bond dollar.

Overcalls and Loans

The partnership agreement may provide that in addition to the amount that the limited partners are investing, they may be called upon to make an additional investment up to 10 percent, or sometimes up to 15 or 20 percent of the amount of their original investment. This is known as an overcall.

In the event that additional money is needed above the total capitalization (and above the overcall if it is provided for in the agreement) the general partner or others may furnish this money and may do so as a loan that may be entitled to be repaid prior to the return of any of the contributions of the limited partners. It is usually provided that the partnership cannot incur any expenses in connection with any such loan, nor can the percentage of the limited partners' profits be affected by such an arrangement. It is for the general partner to reimburse the person for the loan.

Option Provisions in Agreement

It is most usual for a partnership agreement to contain the provisions of the option agreement, particularly the amount that was spent for the option, the terms of the option, and the arrangement with respect to subsidiary rights. Having discussed subsidiary rights in connection with the option agreement, we know that this term, commonly used, refers to not only the right to produce the play in other places and in other media, but is used, as well, to refer to the production's interest in the profits that accrue to the author from the sale or other disposition of the subsidiary rights.

Termination of Partnership

It is provided in the agreement that the partnership will terminate when all rights in the play have been exhausted, or upon the death, retirement, or insanity of an individual general partner or the dissolution of a corporate general partner. Upon termination of the partnership, the agreement will provide that all of the bills will first be paid, and then a reserve will be established for payment of any bills that accrue later. Thereafter, the limited partners will first have the amount of their respective investment returned to them, and if there is any money left over, it will be shared in the same percentage that the general partners and the limited partners share the profits of the company; that is, usually with the limited partners receiving 50 percent and the general partners receiving the other 50 percent.

Miscellaneous

Of course, there are some other standard provisions that usually appear in partnership agreements. We've already discussed an arbitration clause with respect to an option, and the limited partnership agreement will also contain such a provision. The agreement may be executed in counterparts (each investor signs a separate document), all of which taken together are deemed one original, and there will be a statement to this effect in the agreement. This means that all of the parties need not sign the same copy of the agreement.

The agreement will also provide that the limited partners grant a general partner a power of attorney to sign the Certificate of Limited Partnership, any amended certificate and the Certificate of Dissolution of the Partnership, so that no matter how many limited partners there are, the Certificate of Limited Partnership, which must be filed with the County Clerk, need not personally be signed by each of these limited partners. The Certificate of Limited Partnership will be filed as soon as front money is raised and will be amended thereafter when new front money investors come in, and finally when the total production budget is raised. It should be a totally unnecessary chore to have the certificate and each amendment signed by each investor.

A limited partnership agreement sometimes provides that in the event the producer wants to produce an additional company of the play, such as a touring or a London production, he may retain the profits from the original company over and above the reserve, until he has accumulated enough money to produce the additional company. If the profits are used for this purpose, it will in effect mean that the investors in the original company will become investors in the additional company with their profits from the original company.

Bear in mind that the partnership agreement is prepared prior to a producer's raising any money. The actual formation of the partnership usually takes place at the time that the Certificate of Limited Partnership is filed with the County Clerk.

CHAPTER 4

Raising the Money

THE OPTION HAS BEEN negotiated and prepared—you've signed it, parted with some of your own money, may also have a co-producer, and now own a property. You have six months or a year in which to do all of the things necessary to get the play on stage for your opening night. Your most pressing concern now becomes "money."

If you have an attractive can of beans, there is always a purchaser for it. I do know of instances where very successful shows have had long, hard struggles to raise the necessary production money; however, there is always the consolation that most good scripts do eventually get the necessary money and do get produced. Worse than not getting the money is seeing a production that has raised its money badly produced. If a play, a person, a book, or a movie does not live up to its potential, it is heartbreaking.

BUDGETS

Raising money involves a number of things, and before we can intelligently consider this, it is necessary to obtain budgets so that we know how much has to be raised and how it will be spent. You will need a preproduction budget that will set forth the total amount of money necessary to produce the play including the reserve, and you will need a weekly budget that will set forth the anticipated usual expenses during each week. The weekly budget will make it easy to determine what percentage of the theatre must be sold each week in order for you to break even, and what the potential profit would be if the show does "sold out" business.

The preproduction budget for an Off-Broadway show is in all probability going to be between $100,000 and $350,000. If it is substantially less than $100,000, you probably made a mistake in your computations. If it is substantially more than $350,000, you had better worry a second time about whether or not you want to produce the show. Equally, or maybe even more, important is the weekly budget. If the preproduction budget is a little excessive it can be compensated for if the weekly running expenses are relatively low in comparison to the potential weekly gross box office receipts. The potential net profits is really the important item in determining whether the preproduction budget can be recouped.

After preparing the weekly budget, if you see that the production does not break even at about 50 percent or 60 percent of capacity, again you'd better either recompute the budget or start looking for a different property. The concept of sold-out houses is a nice idea to envision, but it happens so rarely in the business that a producer is wise in assuming that if the production is doing 75 percent or 80 percent of capacity, it is doing well. Even a smash hit is rarely sold-out for every performance every night of the week unless it's in an extremely small theatre. It's just that there are certain nights during the week, such as Tuesday or Wednesday, and rainy or snowy nights, when the demand is less, and then, too, some of the less-desirable seats are sometimes hard to sell.

In all probability, the budgets you have prepared will show that the total amount invested may be recovered if the production does sold-out business for between eight and sixteen weeks. If your figures are considerably different than this, once again recompute or consider abandoning the project.

If you have never seen a budget, take a look at the example of a budget for a musical, in Appendix C. To learn how to prepare a budget, it is strongly urged that you make contact with a good general manager—there are several in the business—and you will need one eventually anyhow. In a later chapter there is a more detailed discussion of the general manager and his duties. A general manager will be able to prepare the budgets for you that you will need, and you will be able to relax knowing that they are prepared as they should be.

TYPICAL BUDGETS (EXAMPLES)

So that you have some idea of what a budget looks like, there is set forth in Appendix C typical budgets for an Off-Broadway musical play and typical budgets for an Off-Broadway musical review performed in a cabaret theatre. Please again bear in mind that these are not average budgets since there is no such thing as an average budget. Also bear in mind that many of the items on a budget change weekly or monthly, and those items that don't change weekly or monthly could have changed since these budgets were prepared.

How to raise the money for the show is an easy question for me to answer, "I don't know." Some people try backers' auditions; they sometimes work. Some people try friends; that sometimes works. Some people send out copies of the script; that sometimes works. Some people try a combination of these; that sometimes works. What works for you, you will have to discover after you attempt to raise the money and examine the results.

BACKERS' AUDITIONS

Some backers' auditions provide potential investors with a sampling of the play. The audition may take place in someone's home, in a hotel room rented for that purpose, or in some other public place such as a restaurant. Since any money spent to raise money must come from the producer and is not reimbursable to him, his circumstances may govern the lavishness of the backers' auditions. The Belasco Room at Sardi's has become a favorite auditioning place; however, some Off-Broadway producers do not have the money to spend on so elaborate an audition. The suite of the Dramatists Guild, Inc., atop the Sardi's building is sometimes used for backers' auditions. You may plan on serving alcoholic beverages or coffee and cake. Nice surroundings may be helpful in getting people to part with their money and perhaps the drinks may also help; however, nothing is quite as important as what happens on stage.

The backers' audition may consist of actors performing the parts, or as is often done with musicals, the author may give the story line, and the composer and author sing the musical numbers.

While I'm not sure whether serving alcoholic beverages is more important than serving coffee, I am nevertheless quite sure of two things. First, you should start on time. It's unfair to the people who arrive on time to be kept waiting. When you want people to invest in a show, it's advisable not to get them angry with a wait. If you are serving drinks, however, it's all right to allow a half hour for the drinks before the presentation, but a half hour doesn't mean forty-five minutes or an hour.

Second, the presentation should not be more than an hour or an hour and fifteen minutes. Some producers find it hard to cut a play as they are so certain that every line is important. This is especially true if the author is the producer. Backers who come to backers' auditions, for the most part, do not want to sit through the entire play but will settle for a condensed version.

Before or after the presentation, the producer usually makes a short speech in which he tells a little bit about himself, about the budget, and answers any questions that might come up. This presentation by the producer also must be short. Short means not more than five or six minutes.

Don't count on very many people at the conclusion of the audition pulling out their checkbooks and writing you a check. It doesn't happen very often that they do. What should happen is that, within two or three days after the audition, you will follow up each one of the people who attended by telephoning them to see if they are interested in investing in the play. This means, of course, that you must have taken the names, addresses, and telephone numbers of all of the people who attended the audition. If you have interested people who want to invest, of course you must question them about any friends they have who might be interested and whom you could invite to the next audition.

There are occasions when producers will send out large mailings from mailing lists that they have assembled or purchased. The mailing lists usually consist of people who have previously invested in shows. For the most part, this method of raising money is not to be recommended. You will find that you may get people to backers' auditions because they are curious, are seeking entertainment, and have nothing else to do that evening. Let's face the fact that most people—not all, mind you—invest in shows because of some personal connection with it, in some way. They either know the producer, the author, the star, or a friend of theirs knows someone who is part of the show. There is usually some kind of a personal involvement on the part of most Off-

Broadway investors rather than the investment coming as a business venture.

You will have to decide how small an investment you will be willing to accept. If 1 percent of the show sells for $4,000—that is, if you have a $200,000 budget—you will probably be willing to accept an investment for one-half percent at $2,000. Many producers will bother with investments in any reasonable amount and would certainly consider $1,000 to be a reasonable amount.

It must appear evident that I can't say for certain how you should raise the money. I do, however, know what you must do *before* you can raise the money. Which, of course, brings us to a discussion of the Securities and Exchange Commission and the Attorney General of the State of New York.

THE SECURITIES AND EXCHANGE COMMISSION

I really think I spoke too soon when I previously commented that no subject is surrounded with so much confusion as "subsidiaries." I do believe, upon reflection, that the requirements of the Securities and Exchange Commission, which is usually referred to as the "SEC," often elicit even more confusion. This should not be so, because the SEC regulations and SEC requirements setting forth whether or not SEC filing is necessary are not really that complicated. The SEC regulates the issuance, or sale, of securities. Although a security is commonly thought of as a stock or a bond, the sale of a limited partnership interest in a producing company organized to produce a play is considered a sale of a "security." Although the requirements as to the necessity for a filing are not that complicated, an SEC filing itself is somewhat complicated. Since producers want to avoid the trouble, time, and expense of a filing if they can, they are too often ready to believe anything they might hear that would serve as an excuse for them not to file with the SEC.

If you intend to raise money outside the state of New York; that is, if you intend to go to, send mail to, telephone, or in any other way approach someone in a state other than the state of New York to raise money, and if this consists of a public offering, then you must file with the SEC. A *public offering* means exactly what it sounds like it means. It means that you are offering to sell an interest in the limited partnership (or other entity) that will be producing the play to people you don't know or people you haven't known. It means someone other than sophisticated investors, who may be your intimate friends or your business associates. And furthermore, if there is any question as to whether or not your offering constitutes a "public" offering, the presumptions the SEC makes support the conclusion that it is a public offering.

When the chap across the hall tells you that you need not file with the SEC if you have less than nine investors, don't believe him. When your wife's cousin tells you that you needn't file with the SEC if your production budget is less than $60,000, don't believe him. When your actor friend, who just produced a show down in the Village tells you that there is a way to avoid filing with the SEC if you give the New Jersey resident who's going to invest the money a New York residence for the purpose of the agreement, don't believe him. It's hardly worth the risk, in view of the fact that, among other possible penalties, if you raise money in interstate commerce by a public offering and you do not file with the SEC, you, as the producer, are personally liable for the money you have raised. Understand that that means you may raise the full $300,000, open your show, get bombed by the reviews, close the show, and then have to reach into your pocket and come up with $300,000 to return to the investors. Is this really worth the risk of not filing with the SEC when you should have done so? There are also criminal penalties written into the law and one could end up in jail for securities violations. Some well-known theatrical investors have in fact accomplished just this, ended up in jail.

Since the budget for an Off-Broadway production would be less than $1½ million, our discussion will be concerned with an "Exemption from Registration under Regulation A" rather than what is known as a full registration. Don't be mislead by the term *Exemption from Registration.* The term is somewhat misleading because one might assume that if you are "exempt" there is nothing you need do. This, of course, is not the case. Registration is a complicated procedure, so the exemption is a concession. You must file certain documents with the SEC that they will accept for filing in order for you to obtain your exemption from registration.

Filing for an Exemption

What must one file with the SEC? One must file four copies of a "Notification under Regulation A," which is a document that gives certain information about you as the issuer. The notification will state where you will be conducting business, information on persons with whom you are affiliated, the name of your counsel, whether or not you have ever been convicted of a crime or guilty of a post-office fraud, whether you have been declared a bankrupt, as well as any connection you may have with underwriters, the states in which you intend to raise money, information on any other offerings by you during the last year, and any other offerings contemplated by you. This document will be prepared by your attorney and will be signed by you, and four copies will be submitted to the SEC, together with four copies of your proposed offering circular, four copies of your proposed limited partnership agreement, four copies of all sales material you intend to use, and four copies each of other pertinent documents. Depending upon how busy the SEC is, within four to six weeks after the submission of this material to them, a letter will be forwarded to your attorney informing him or her of either the acceptance as filed or the changes requested by the SEC before they will accept the submissions for filing.

You will notice that I referred to an "acceptance" for filing rather than an "approval" of filing. The Securities and Exchange Commission is careful to make this important distinction in that they do not approve or disapprove of the filing. They accept what is submitted for filing or they may reject it. In effect, if it does not meet with their approval, they will not accept it for filing, although they are careful to point out that they do not ever officially approve of what is filed.

Offering Circular

You may not use any written material in connection with the offering that has not been filed with the SEC. You must give an offering circular to each prospective investor. Sometimes a producer tries to be clever and surreptitiously prepares an attractive brochure that has not been filed with the SEC and that he mails or distributes together with the offering circular. Every client of mine knows not to do this, and on the one occasion when a client, without my knowledge, sneaked something into a large mailing and it was discovered, the consequences were not pleasant. Again, it's easier to properly file with the SEC than to run the risk of not filing if it is required or to avoid the SEC requirements.

The offering circular that must be filed with the SEC for an exemption from registration is patterned after a form that was arrived at as a result of discussions between the SEC and the League of New York Theatres (now known as the American League of Theatres and Producers). The offering circular presently used leaves much to be desired, from a theatrical point of view, but is a great improvement over the offering circular previously used. The former offering circular had no relationship to theatre but was originally intended for use by almost every other type of business, such as oil companies, steel companies, and the like.

The SEC takes the position that they merely want a full and fair disclosure of all pertinent information and that nothing must be misleading. The offering circular now in use certainly could not be considered a document that would encourage investment in a theatrical production. Be that as it may, the offering circular explains some of the terms of the limited partnership agreement, such as the division of profits and the fact that the producers will receive a percentage of the net profits without making a financial contribution. It sets forth the risk to the investors, and includes statistics on the percentage of plays during the previous season that resulted in losses to investors; the experience of the producers; the minimum number of performances that the play will have to run in order to recover the initial investment; and what percentage of plays actually ran this long during the previous season. There is additional information on the compensation of the general partners, as well as a preproduction budget setting forth how the proceeds of the offering will be used. There is a provision setting forth the estimated weekly budget and what precentage of the gross weekly box office receipts and of the net receipts will first be paid as expenses off the top to stars, the director, etc., before there are net profits. The offering circular also contains a short discussion of the subsidiary rights and the fact that the investors will receive financial statements.

A typical example of an offering circular for an Off-Broadway play appears in Appendix D.

We have already discussed the Limited Partnership agreement that must be filed with the offering circular and the Notification under Regulation A, but it should be noted that four copies of it must be filed with the other documents.

There are also provisions for a private offering exemption pursuant to Regulation D. This is a much simpler procedure and, like Regulation A, requires that you comply with the various state securities laws that may be applicable. There are limitations in Regulation D designed to make certain that the prospective investors are knowledgeable and financially secure enough to run the risk inherent in the investment.

Although the SEC does not pass upon the merits of any security, nor the accuracy or the completeness of an offering circular or any other selling literature (and you will note that this is stated in bold type on the first page of the sample offering circular in Appendix D), nevertheless, I strongly urge that you as producer make certain of the accuracy and completeness of any offering circular or selling literature that you use. It's just as easy—in fact easier—to be honest. Dishonesty is not only bad business, it's bad theatre.

THE ATTORNEY GENERAL

You must satisfy the Arts and Cultural Affairs Law of the state of New York and the regulations promulgated thereunder if you intend to raise money in the state of New York. If you are raising money only in the state of New York you can avoid an SEC filing. If you have filed with the SEC, and if you have included the several things in your offering literature required by the Arts and Cultural Affairs Law and the Regulations, then your filing with the Attorney General is simplified, you just furnish the Attorney General with copies of the documents that were accepted for filing by the Securities and Exchange Commission.

It should be noted that most, if not all, of the states of the Union, have requirements similar to our New York State Theatre Financing Regulations governing a filing with a state office before one may offer a security interest for sale. The state laws governing security issues are known as "Blue Sky" laws. You may remember that one of the items of information contained in the Notification under Regulation A furnished to the SEC is a statement setting forth in which states you intend to raise money. It also may be necessary to file in each of these states. Some states have exemptions from filing based on the number to whom the offering is made, the number to whom a sale is made, or some other arbitrary standard. Consult your attorney, who will advise you as to what filings are necessary and where you must file.

In the case of a filing solely with the Attorney General, if the offering is less than $250,000, you have your choice of filing both a prospectus (an offering circular) and a limited partnership agreement; or you may simply file the limited partnership agreement if it sets forth all of the terms of the agreement you have with the limited partners. Because the agreement should set forth all of such terms, I usually advise my clients to forgo the offering circular and to confine the filing to the limited partnership agreement. The offering circular required by the Attorney General is an added expense and, like the SEC offering circular, requires the kind of language that is not that helpful in raising money. Again, with the SEC you have no choice but to use an offering circular; however, if it is a filing solely with the Attorney General you have a choice, and I recommend against the use of the offering circular.

If the offering is made to fewer than thirty-six persons, you may avoid any filing with the Attorney General. To accomplish this, however, each of the investors must expressly waive, in writing, the right to have offering literature filed with the Attorney General and the right to receive information that would be contained in such an offering circular. Take note that the offering may only be made to fewer than thirty-six persons, not sold to fewer than thirty-six persons. The distinction between offerees and purchasers must always be borne in mind when dealing with securities laws.

One should also bear in mind that it is not necessary to file with the Attorney General if the offer is made to less than five persons, with the sole purpose of obtaining front money, for the purposes noted in the discussion of front money in Chapter 2.

INVESTMENT PROCEDURE

The producer generally passes out copies of the limited partnership agreement with the offering circular if an offering circular is used. If someone wants to invest in a show, the procedure is simple. The party signs the agreement in one of the two or three places provided for and delivers the partnership agreement, together with the check, to the producer. The limited partnership agreement usually provides that a person may sign as a limited partner or may in signing give the producer permission to use the money prior to the total budget being raised. In some agreements, there is also a provision to the effect that the investor who signs may be making an investment other than in cash.

Actually, the money that the investor is investing is almost always turned over to the producer at the time the limited partnership agreement is signed; however, the agreement may be signed by the investor and the money delivered to the producer later on demand.

Starting the Company

It is important that the producer's attorney file a Certificate of Limited Partnership as soon as any money has been invested that will be used for the production, without waiting until the total production budget is raised. Front money may be used ahead of time and investors may give written permission to the use of their funds prior to capitalization. It is important to give those investors the protection of limited liability. Unless the filing is done noting them as limited partners, they would share the general partner's liability with the general partner.

From time to time, if other investors authorize prior use of their funds, the certificate is amended and filed to include them as limited partners. When the total production budget is raised, the certificate is amended again to include all of the investors in the filed documents.

The Certificate of Limited Partnership mentioned previously is a document that sets forth some of the terms of the partnership—that is, the terms with respect to the business of the partnership and the respective interests of the general partners and the limited partners. It must also contain the names, addresses, and amount of the investment of each partner. The certificate, or digest thereof, must be published once a week for six consecutive weeks, in two newspapers in the county where the filing takes place. However, if the title of the partnership includes the words *Limited Partnership,* and it is a stage theatrical production company, the publication is not required. This would mean a considerable savings in money if there were many partners. The producing company is in business as a limited partnership when the certificate is filed, and everything you were doing for the play as an individual or as a joint venture now becomes the business of the partnership. You will assign all of the agreements to the company. The limited partnership assumes all of the obligations of all of the contracts and takes all of the benefits of the same contracts.

The attorney for the production will prepare a "conformed" copy of the partnership agreement. A conformed copy is an exact copy in which all of the names of the general partners and the limited partners are listed at the end, in the same fashion that they have signed the agreement. One of these is then sent to each investor.

At this time, you will reimburse yourself for all properly recoupable expenses made by you for the producing company. The money spent by you to option the property, for legal expenses, and for other items you've given to the company that are properly budgeted items is reimbursable to you. *You may not reimburse yourself for money spent to raise money.* Backers' auditions and everything connected with them are the expense of the producer and not the producing company.

You should bear in mind that front money furnished by you or someone else may be considered an investment in the producing company to the extent that the money is used for the company and is not returned to the person who furnishes the front money. But to the extent that front money is used for backers' auditions or other money raising, it cannot be considered an investment in the producing company.

CHAPTER 5

Obtaining a Theatre

A LTHOUGH YOU CAN'T REALLY start negotiating for a theatre until you know exactly when the money will be raised, as the theatre situation changes daily, at the time you prepared the budget, you should have given consideration to the size of the theatre you want and can afford. Naturally, the smaller houses cost less, and furthermore, the theatres of 199 seats or fewer have different union requirements than the larger theatres. Also, each of the unions has minimums based on the number of seats in the theatre, usually 100–199, 200–299, 300–399, 400–499. Actors' Equity is the exception, making the division based on seating of 100–199, 200–250, 251–299, 300–350, 351–499.

You next speak with the theatre owners or the managers of the theatres in which you are interested, to find out what theatres are available and which will fit into your budget requirements. After you settle on the theatre and the budget is raised, you start negotiations in earnest on the terms that will be part of the license agreement of the theatre. If you don't have the total budget raised, but you are close and certain it will be raised, there is nothing to prevent you from using your own money for the purpose of obtaining the license on the theatre. Understand, however, that most Off-Broadway theatres require between three and six weeks' advance deposit or security, and this can be a substantial amount. These payments can be as little as $10,000 or as much as $30,000 or more.

ADVANCE DEPOSIT

Sometimes there are all kinds of deals that can be made with respect to the theatre advance, and when I say all kinds of deals, I mean exactly that. It is possible to negotiate a license agreement which provides that after the production has been in the theatre for a certain number of weeks you may reduce the amount that is held on deposit by playing a week or two or three without paying the license fee that week or two. For an example, the license may provide that after two months you may use up three weeks of the six weeks' deposit the theatre is holding, so that the theatre then will be holding a deposit of only three weeks' rental. The deposit is money that is to be used for the last three, four, five or six weeks of the occupancy of the theatre depending upon the size of the deposit.

FOUR-WALL CONTRACT

The first thing you must find out in your negotiations is whether you are obtaining a "four-wall" contract; that is, are you leasing just the theatre, or the theatre and added personnel. Some theatres require that you not only lease, or license, the theatre, but that you pay them sufficient money to cover the box office help and the ushers as well as the theatre manager and other personnel that the theatre furnishes to you. The New York City Department of Licenses takes the position that the box office personnel must be under the control of the theatre owner, and this kind of an arrangement has some problems in that if the box office personnel, who are directly responsible for the money, are hired by the theatre, then they are responsible to the theatre. But they are handling your money and are dealing with your money so they should in fact be beholden to you.

LEASE OR LICENSE

Most theatre agreements are not a lease but a license agreement. The distinction between a lease and a license is beyond the scope of this book, but for your purposes at this time, the differences are not that material. There is a whole body of landlord-and-tenant law that is a part of the common law and the statutory law, which favors tenants for the most part. For this reason, the landlords use a license agreement to avoid the applicability of that body of law.

The agreement will most likely provide that the theatre is free to license the use of the premises at other hours to other productions; however, they cannot interfere with the production or stage sets and props of the primary occupant at that time. The performance schedule should be the right of the major tenant. As the major tenant, you should not have to work your schedule around any secondary tenants. The most common use of the theatre at other hours is for children's theatre. It is not unusual for a children's theatre group to use an occupied theatre on Saturday morning or Sunday morning to present a show, without interfering with the sets and props that are in place.

RUN OF THE SHOW AND MOVING

The theatre lease or license usually is for the run of the show, which means that the theatre owner cannot put you out of the theatre so long as the play is running, you pay your rent, and comply with the other lease or license terms. By the same token, you must stay in this theatre and cannot move your play to another Off-Broadway theatre unless the theatre for some reason loses its license or for some other reason cannot be occupied. Moving can be very costly, so in most instances one should not anticipate a move. I have had producers come to me with the thought in mind that they would open a show in a particular theatre just because it is available, even though they consider the theatre all wrong for this particular play. The plan proposed is to get those great reviews that they know they will get and immediately move the show to a better house. Don't count on doing this! It really doesn't make sense from a business point of view and is nearly impossible to accomplish. One should also bear in mind that the move from an Off-Broadway house to a Broadway house is very expensive, and the move has rarely proven successful.

Of course, the theatre owner will make a different deal, depending upon how anxious the theatre owner is to have a particular show in that theatre. In fact, under some circumstances, theatre owners will make an investment in the production to the extent of the advance deposit. There have been instances where theatre owners have even been known to invest beyond this, to the extent that they have actually invested money in a show that comes into their theatre.

STOP CLAUSE

Broadway theatre leases have a provision (the "stop clause") stating that if the box office receipts fall below a certain amount of money during any two consecutive weeks, the landlord may ask the production to leave the theatre in order to put another show in. The reason for this is that a Broadway show pays the theatre a percentage of its gross box office receipts as rental. Most Off-Broadway theatres are now insisting on a payment of a percentage of the gross weekly box office receipts and for this reason will expect a stop clause in the license agreement. Unless you are paying a percentage of the gross weekly box office receipts, you should not concede to such a clause, and if you are, it's pretty hard to argue against it.

PAYMENT OF RENT

As mentioned above, almost all Off-Broadway theatres get a percentage of the production's gross weekly box office receipts. In addition, they get a base rent. The participation in box office receipts is sometimes based on receipts above the breakeven point, and in other cases, the theatre will insist upon 5 percent of the gross receipts from the first receipts received, in addition to the base rent.

The most important part of your deal is that you pay the rent. Almost every lease and license agreement is prepared for the benefit of the landlord. At the beginning, it states how much the tenant must pay and at the end it says that if the tenant complies with the terms of the lease, pays his rent, and abides by the rules of the landlord that he may enjoy peaceful possession of the premises. Everything written in between is for the landlord's benefit. In spite of all the onerous provisions of a lease, and some of them are most onerous, as long as you pay your rent, you can't get in too much trouble. The landlord wants to make certain that you do no physical damage to the theatre and that you maintain the premises in reasonably the same condition they were in at the time you took possession; and he wants to make certain that the rent is paid. These are not unreasonable demands.

THEATRE LICENSE AND REHEARSALS

From the point of view of the producer, you should make certain that your lease, license agreement, or whatever provides that the landlord has a theatre license issued by the Department of Licenses, and that he will maintain the theatre license. This is terribly important to you, as it is illegal to perform in front of an audience in a theatre that has no license.

You may be able to negotiate with the landlord to permit you to use the premises for rehearsals at a very reduced rate. It is not unusual to pay $1,000 per week for rehearsals in a theatre where the base rental might be $2,500 a week during performances. It may also be possible for you to negotiate a reduced rate for the theatre during previews. The amount of money that you pay during previews can vary between an amount that is approximately one-half of the usual rental for the theatre and the same amount that is paid during any other paid performances. This is an item for negotiation.

EQUITY REQUIREMENTS

You should make certain that the theatre meets all of the requirements of Actors' Equity Association. There must be separate dressing rooms for men and women; there must be toilet facilities available to the members of the cast, separate from the audience; there must be wash basins with hot and cold running water; there must be a cooler for drinking water; and thirty inches of dressing-table space for each actor. All new theatres built hereafter must be fully air conditioned—that is, the playing area and the dressing room area—and they must have separate sanitary facilities backstage for men and women. Not only should the theatre be equipped with everything that is required by Actors' Equity, but the agreement should provide that the theatre must continue to maintain all of these requirements.

THEATRE DEPOSIT

The lease or license agreement will almost always make provision for a deposit of between $500 and $7,500, or more, to be held by the landlord (or licensor) to insure against breakage, damage to the theatre and telephone or other charges for which the theatre might be held responsible.

MAINTENANCE AND CONCESSIONS

Very few Off-Broadway theatres have lighting or sound equipment, and those that do usually ask for additional payment for the use of their equipment. In renting or licensing a theatre that does have lighting or sound equipment, the producer must always be sure to examine the equipment and see that it is in good working order and suitable for the requirements of the production. If the equipment is suitable, the license fee charged by the theatre for such equipment will usually be much less than what a commercial rental company would charge. Rental of lights and sound equipment are the kind of items that may be overlooked when preparing the budget. Who is responsible for maintenance of the air conditioning should always be clearly set forth in the license agreement.

The producer should try, if possible, to acquire the right to run a concession for the sale of sheet music and records if the play is a musical. Most theatre owners insist on having the right to run all of the concessions and rarely will part with this right, for it means that the theatre will make extra money—from the sale of drinks, checking coats, and the sale of various other items.

ADVERTISING

The landlord may, under certain circumstances, try to obtain some control over the advertising, with particular reference to the way the theatre is mentioned in the ads, including the directions set forth for getting to the theatre. Be careful that you do not let the theatre owner control your ads. I do not believe that is a proper function of the theatre owner, and it will not be in your best interest to have your hands tied in this matter.

REMOVAL OF PROPERTY AT END OF RUN AND HOUSE SEATS

Make certain that you have ample time at the conclusion of the lease or license to remove all of your property.

Some leases and some license agreements provide that the theatre owner may have a certain number of house seats for each performance of the show. Almost all lease or license agreements contain a provision stating that the tenant cannot make any arrangements with any unions contrary to the terms that have already been settled upon between that particular theatre and the different unions.

INSURANCE

The license agreement will certainly provide that you must obtain and maintain general liability insurance and fire insurance which must also protect the theatre owner. It will also provide that the producer obtain public liability insurance, or reimburse the theatre owner for the premiums if paid by the owner. The premiums for such insurance are usually a rate that is fixed, based on multiples of one hundred in the audience. As a matter of fact, you should bear in mind that the following insurance policies are desirable and some are required. You should consider the following:

Box office hold-up and safe burglary insurance

Box office Fidelity Bond

New York State group disability benefits

Payroll hold-up broad form policy (This is desirable if you pay the cast and crew by cash.)

Workmen's Compensation

Theatrical floater for physical props—that is, scenery, costumes, rented
    lighting equipment, sound equipment, and wardrobe

Extraordinary risk (This is an Equity requirement to cover the salary loss
    of Equity personnel due to injuries from acrobatic feats, use of
    weapons, leaps, falls, pyrotechnics, and so forth.)

Your general manager will assist you in obtaining the insurance
necessary and desirable.

ASSIGNABILITY

There is one other provision that should appear in the lease as well
as in any other agreement you enter into if it occurs before the producing company is organized. There must be a provision that you can
assign the lease or other agreement to the limited partnership or other
entity that will later be organized to produce the play. You will remember that we previously discussed an assignment of the option agreement
and that it is not unusual to have a provision limiting the assignment
to a partnership or corporation in which you are one of the principals.
Nor is it unusual to have a provision that you will continue to be
responsible for the lease, that is, that you as well as the producing
company agree to live up to your end of the bargain.

LOCATION

Serious consideration must be given to location of the theatre. I used
to be of the opinion that if you have a good show, people will go
anywhere in the city to see it. In recent years, I've had reason to
question this theory. I do know of several theatres, in unsafe or inaccessible neighborhoods, that have on more than one occasion had good
shows with artistic merit that received good reviews, and, in spite of
this, were not financially successful.

The Greenwich Village area is probably the most likely area for
walk-in trade—that is, people who walk in off the streets to buy tickets.
The success of a theatre building, of course, is judged by the number

of hits and commercially successful shows that have appeared in that theatre. From an artistic point of view, a director may have a different standard for judging a theatre. As the producer of a show, it is important to you that people buy tickets, and the old truism is equally applicable to an Off-Broadway production—namely, that it is not "good theatre" unless there are people watching it.

BARGAINING

Bear in mind that it's easy to make a list of the things that you want in a lease, license, or any other agreement. One does not always get everything one wants in life. You may not get all of the lease or license provisions that you would like. Arranging a lease or license agreement involves negotiation, which means giving and taking. If you are negotiating with a theatre considered to be a more desirable house, then you will be bargaining from weakness, as these theatres are much in demand. Even though you can't always have everything you want in the lease, it is helpful to know what you ought to get and what you are giving up.

VARIETY OF THEATRES

The variety of theatres that one may choose from Off-Broadway in New York City is great. There are proscenium theatres, theatres-in-the-round, three-quarters in the round, and some cabarets have been converted to theatres. Almost all of the Off-Broadway houses today have adequate heat in the winter time and adequate air conditioning during the summer. There was a time not so long ago when the Off-Broadway theatres lacked the comforts that most theatregoers have learned to expect.

CHAPTER 6

Cast, Crew, and Personnel

T HE THEATRE YOU SELECT IS EXTREMELY IMPORTANT. The property you select is terribly important. The selection of the people who will be working in and on the show is also vitally important. I can't and won't say that any one thing or person is more important than any other. Everyone knows for sure that raising the money is important, for without the money you would not be selecting a property, a theatre, or personnel. I have participated in discussions into the wee hours of the night as to whether the director is more important than the star, or whether the stage manager is more important than the set designer. This is utter nonsense. They are all critically important and it behooves you to select all wisely for therein may lie the difference between a flop and a smash hit.

THE DIRECTOR

Let's hope that, by the time you obtain the property, you will have given some serious thought to whom you would like to direct the play. In fact, right after you acquire the property, as soon as you can, you should find yourself a director. Very often there is a great deal of preproduction work for the director to do, and it is sometimes necessary that the play be rewritten. The director is the natural person to work with the playwright to supervise and assist with the rewriting if it is required. If there is no necessity for rewriting immediately after you acquire the property, relax and rest assured that by the time the curtain goes up on opening night, there will have been some changes in the script. Chances are that the director will assist you not only in working with the author on rewrites, but will also help you raise the money by staging backers' auditions if you need them.

Just as you are the chief with respect to the entire show, and especially with the running of the business end of the show, you should select a director in whom you have confidence, so that he or she can be in charge of what happens on stage artistically. Actually, if you're not happy with the director's work, you can, of course, (and your agreement should provide that you can) get another director. However, you should never lose sight of the fact that you are the producer and not the director. If you want to direct the show, do so, but don't do it until you have had an opportunity to read further on about conflicts of interest and other problems that may arise when a producer takes on the director's job.

Before hiring the director you want, be sure that you have discussed, and both agreed upon, in detail all of the artistic aspects of the play. You will then sign the Minimum Basic Agreement for Off-Broadway, which is a collective bargaining agreement between the Society of Stage Directors and Choreographers and the League of Off-Broadway Theatres and Producers. All members of the League are therefore signatories to the agreement. Non-League members must post a security bond (equal to the contractual fee and advance), League members (unless the producer has a history of default with the Society) are not required to post a bond.

The Society of Stage Directors and Choreographers Minimum Basic Contract for Off-Broadway provides that the minimum fee and advance against royalties be no less than the amounts in the table opposite.

In addition to the basic fee and advance, the director will be paid a minimum royalty payment in the amount of 2 percent of the gross weekly box office receipts. Gross weekly box office receipts are defined in the agreement.

The agreement also provides that the director will have the option to direct other productions of the show at not less than the original contractual fee and advance or the applicable SSDC minimum for each production, whichever is greater.

In spite of the minimum provisions that are often applicable, there are some "star directors" who will demand and receive a great deal

For the DIRECTOR

[*To June 30, 1988*]

CATEGORY:	A	B	C	D
(Seating)	(400–499)	(300–399)	(200–299)	(100–199)
FEE:	$4,750	$4,125	$3,375	$2,625
ADVANCE:	1,750	1,375	1,125	875
TOTAL:	$6,500	$5,500	$4,500	$3,500

[*July 1, 1988 To June 30, 1989*]

	A	B	C	D
FEE:	$4,750	$4,125	$3,375	$2,625
ADVANCE:	2,250	1,625	1,375	1,125
TOTAL:	$7,000	$5,750	$4,750	$3,750

[*July 1, 1989 To June 30, 1990*]

	A	B	C	D
FEE:	$4,750	$4,125	$3,375	$2,625
ADVANCE:	2,750	1,875	1,625	1,375
TOTAL:	$7,500	$6,000	$5,000	$4,000

[*July 1, 1990 To June 30, 1991*]

	A	B	C	D
FEE:	$5,250	$4,500	$3,750	$3,000
ADVANCE:	2,750	2,000	1,750	1,500
TOTAL:	$8,000	$6,500	$5,500	$4,500

NOTE: Choreographer at 80% of Director.
Director/Choreographer at 175% of Director.

Payable 50% on signing of the contract, 25% on the first day of rehearsal, and 25% on the first day of the third week of rehearsal. All of these payments are deemed nonreturnable.

more than the minimums. The amounts often depend on what the director's agent feels the traffic will bear.

Billing credits are always a problem. Like the author, the director will often ill-advisedly insist that his or her name be the largest name on the program, in the ad, or wherever billing credits are given. This may prevent the producer from getting a star who would be most desirable for the part.

A provision that the director may have the option to direct future productions is all right as long as it is confined solely to future productions over which this producer has some control, and the agreement must so provide.

THE CAST

The cast is selected by the director with the assistance of the producer and the approval of the author. The stage manager assists with the auditions and very often contributes his advice. The job basically ought to be the director's and although you as the producer will be hiring the cast and should be satisfied, unless you have strong objections to anyone, you ought to give the director a good deal of leeway to exercise his judgment. You should have selected a director you have faith in and trust, and this being a very important part of his job is part of the reason that you hired him. Just make certain that your motivation as well as the director's for casting a particular person is consistent with what is in the best interest of the play. Hiring with the help of a casting couch is not recommended.

The Actors' Equity Association Contract

The Actors' Equity Association Off-Broadway Contract, *effective November 2, 1987,* provides that the Actor's minimum weekly salary shall be based on the size of theatre (from Category A, the smallest, to Category E, the largest) and the gross weekly box office receipts:

	CATEGORY	A	B	C	D	E
Level	Gross	(100–199)	(200–250)	(251–299)	(300–350)	(351–499)
(1)	$ 0–22,500	$260	$315	$365	$435	$490
(2)	22,501–25,000	310	335	365	435	490
(3)	25,001–30,000	365	370	385	435	490
(4)	30,001–35,000	405	415	420	450	490
(5)	35,001–40,000	435	440	445	465	490
(6)	40,001–45,000	455	460	465	480	500
(7)	45,001–50,000	465	470	480	500	510
(8)	50,001–55,000	475	480	495	515	520
(9)	Over 55,000	480	490	515	525	530

These minimum rates will be in effect through October 30, 1988. There is an increase in the minimum (Level #1) salary commencing the Monday following the last Sunday in October of each year. The current Equity Off-Broadway Contract will expire on October 28, 1990.

In addition to the salary payments, payments are also made to the Equity-League Pension and Health Funds. A weekly payment of 8 percent of the Equity payroll to the Equity-League Pension Fund, and a weekly payment for hospitalization and medical insurance for each Equity employee in the amount of $43.00 for productions in theatres seating up to 299; and for productions in theatres seating 300 or more: $47.91 to June 26, 1988; $53.74 to June 25, 1989; $60.28 to June 24, 1990; and $66.91 to October 28, 1990. There is also a payment for salary-continuance insurance added to the health payment, currently 85 cents, which will not increase to more than $1.50 through October 28, 1990.

An actor will receive an additional $10 after every 32 weeks of employment in a show.

The maximum weekly rehearsal time for an actor in a show after opening is eight hours (twelve hours for understudies), without payment of overtime (currently $9 an hour or part thereof, increasing to $9.50 after October 30, 1988, and $10 after October 29, 1989), and no rehearsal is permitted on days when a show has two performances.

The standard termination notice period for Equity members is two weeks, however, if both parties agree, this period can be for up to four weeks without an increase of the minimum salary. For a period of more than four weeks, actors must be signed to a limited run-of-the-play contract and an additional incremental payment added to their minimum salary, with the amount of the additional increment determined by the size (category) of theatre in which the production is playing, and the length of the notice period: up to three months from first performance, or up to six months.

CATEGORY:	A	B	C	D	E
3-Month R.O.P.	$100	100	90	80	70
6-Month R.O.P.	$190	160	125	100	100

A condition of the Equity Off-Broadway Agreement that you should be familiar with is "more remunerative employment": an actor may absent him/herself from the show with only seven days' notice for up to three weeks for more remunerative employment in the entertainment industry, and with only ten days' notice for more remunerative employment of more than three weeks. The more-remunerative-employment provisions of the contract are not available to the actor signed to a run-of-the-play contract.

In spite of the Equity minimum, there are occasions when you will pay a particular star as much as $1,000 a week in the smaller theatres and as much as $2,000 or more in the largest. What's more, such an extravagance might be money well spent. Almost always, however, the cast is hired for the Equity minimum and their greater remuneration comes from the opportunity to work and the exposure that it brings.

THE STAGE MANAGER

Selection of a good stage manager is a most important job. Prior to and after opening, the stage manager is responsible for the coordination of everything that happens onstage and backstage, including the proper lighting as designed by the lighting designer, any recordings that must be played, all off-stage noises, and any slide projection or film strips that may be required. The stage manager is exactly what the name implies, that is, the manager of the stage and, as such, is in charge of all items as well as all people on the stage. The importance of the stage manager cannot possibly be over-emphasized.

All script changes must go through the stage manager, who is responsible for light cues, sound cues, actors' cues, and is, in addition to all this, the director's right hand. It is the stage manager's duty to make certain that the sets are changed properly, that the props are all where they should be, that the actors and actresses make their entrances on time. All of the backstage detail and leg work that must be done is handled by or supervised by the stage manager—sometimes after instructions from the director, but sometimes on his or her own initiative.

After the show has opened, in the absence of the director, the stage manager assumes the role of the director, and is able to call rehearsals, do replacement casting, and direct the rehearsals. The stage manager's job begins before rehearsals commence and ends a few weeks after the show closes.

The stage manager, an assistant stage manager, who may also act or understudy (productions with three or fewer actors may request a waiver of the requirement to have an assistant stage manager), and a dance captain (required for productions with a choreographer) are paid a higher minimum than an actor, the amount of the additional minimum salary is determined by the size (category) of theatre in which the production is playing.

CATEGORY:	A	B	C	D	E
Stage Manager:	$70	80	90	100	110
Asst. Stg. Mgr.:	$10	10	10	10	10
ASM (Act or U/S):	$35	40	45	50	55
Dance Captain:	$35	40	45	50	55

SET, COSTUME, AND LIGHTING DESIGNERS

You will also have to make some contractual arrangements with your set designer, costume designer, and lighting designer. In some instances the sets, costumes, and lights are all done by one person, and in other instances you may use two or three people. In all events the set designer creates the designs for, and is usually responsible for the execution and construction of, the sets.

There is no collective bargaining agreement with the union that represents theatrical scenic, costume, and lighting designers—United Scenic Artists Local 829. The producer is under no obligation to engage any union designers; however, if a designer who is a member of the union is engaged, then the Off-Broadway Theatre Contract promulgated by the United Scenic Artists will be required by the union for that scenic, costume, and/or lighting designer, and the designer must receive not less than the minimum fee and "additional weekly compensation" required by the union. The contract also requires the producer to pay to the United Scenic Artists Pension and Welfare Funds an amount equal to eleven (11%) percent of all compensation (other than reimbursement) paid to the designer.

The current minimum rates of compensation required by the union are based on the size of theatre, the design category, the nature (dramatic or musical) of the production, and the number of designs required (see tables on pages 74 and 75).

The agreed-upon fee is paid (net of payroll tax deductions) to the union immediately following the contract signing. The payment of the additional weekly compensation is made to the designer on or before the Friday following each performance week, and may be prorated for weeks where fewer than eight performances are given.

In addition to direct compensation, many designers require than the producer engage an assistant for the designer for a specified minimum

LARGER THEATRES			effective 9/86
Seating:	499–400	399–350	349–300

SCENIC DESIGNER			
Dramatic			
Single Set	$ 2,950.00	$ 2,595.00	$ 2,255.00
Multi Set	4,290.00	3,775.00	3,280.00
Unit Set w/Phases	5,365.00	4,720.00	4,155.00
Musical			
Single Set	$ 2,950.00	$ 2,595.00	$ 2,255.00
Multi Set	9,655.00	8,495.00	7,385.00
Unit Set w/Phases	5,365.00	4,720.00	4,155.00

COSTUME DESIGNER			
Dramatic			
1–3	$ 1,610.00	$ 1,415.00	$ 1,230.00
4–7	+ 133.00 ea.	+ 118.00 ea.	+ 102.00 ea.
8–15	2,680.00	2,360.00	2,050.00
16–20	+ 133.00 ea.	+ 118.00 ea.	+ 102.00 ea.
21–30	3,755.00	3,305.00	2,875.00
31–35	+ 133.00 ea.	+ 118.00 ea.	+ 102.00 ea.
36 +	4,825.00	4,250.00	3,690.00

COSTUME DESIGNER			
Musical			
1–15	$ 3,220.00	$ 2,835.00	$ 2,575.00
16–20	+ 161.00 ea.	+ 141.00 ea.	+ 123.00 ea.
21–30	6,435.00	5,665.00	4,920.00
31–35	+ 161.00 ea.	+ 141.00 ea.	+ 123.00 ea.
36 +	9,655.00	8,500.00	7,385.00

LIGHTING DESIGNER			
Dramatic			
Single Set	$ 1,825.00	$ 1,605.00	$ 1,395.00
Multi Set	2,685.00	2,360.00	2,050.00
Unit Set w/Phases	3,435.00	3,020.00	2,625.00
Musical			
Single Set	2,145.00	1,885.00	1,640.00
Multi Set	4,825.00	4,250.00	3,690.00
Unit Set w/Phases	3,218.00	2,835.00	2,460.00

number of weeks. The union requires that a member designer working as an assistant designer be engaged on a union contract and receive a minimum of $440 per week.

Although there is a union for sound designers (a local of IATSE) and many of the sound designers who work Off-Broadway belong to the union, there is neither a collective bargaining agreement or a promulgated contract.

The amount of fee and royalty, if any, is determined by the extent of the sound design services required. There is a big difference between the design work required for a show with a few sound effects and some music to be played on a tape deck in a smaller theatre, and that required for a musical in a larger theatre. Generally, the sound designer's fee includes specifying the sound equipment required for the show (including the intercom system and/or dressing room monitor/speaker system, if needed), finding and recording the sound effects and/or music required, supervising the installation of the equipment in the theatre and setting the sound cues. Fees generally range from $500 to $5,000; royalties, when appropriate, are generally a fixed sum and range from $25 a week to $100 a week (for a musical in a larger theatre, occasionally a percentage royalty is agreed to, generally ¼ to ½ of 1 percent of the weekly gross box office receipts).

If you have just a few sound effects and/or music on tape, your stage

ADDITIONAL WEEKLY COMPENSATION

	1st thru 5th week	*6th thru 15th week*	*16th week on*
300–499 Seats:	$55.00	$65.00	$75.00

SMALLER THEATRES

Seating:	299–200	199–100
SCENIC DESIGNER		
Basic Set/Unit Set	$1,540	$915
2nd Set/Phase	275	195
Set/Phase after 2nd	155	80
COSTUME DESIGNER		
10 or less	$1,375	$915
11–25, each	55	50
Over 25, each	40	35
LIGHTING DESIGNER		
Single/Unit Set	$1,375	$915
If more than 1 Set/Phase	225	110

ADDITIONAL WEEKLY COMPENSATION

	1st thru 5th week	*6th thru 15th week*	*16th week on*
200–299 Seats:	$45.00	$55.00	$65.00
100–199 Seats:	$35.00	$45.00	$55.00

manager or assistant stage manager may be able to provide all the sound
design work you need, for a very modest payment.

PRESS AGENT

Your press agent will handle all the press releases for the show, will
arrange for television and radio interviews for the stars and other
members of the cast and crew, and will do everything possible to keep
the name of the show and its principals in the public eye. It's a very
important job. As later noted, if you are in a theatre with over 200 seats,
you must have an ATPAM press agent and company manager, and if
you are in a theatre that has under 200 seats, one or the other must
belong to ATPAM. In the smaller house you will probably choose to
have the press agent as an ATPAM member rather than the company
manager.

If the press agent you select is a member of ATPAM, his minimum
fee for an Off-Broadway show will depend upon the number of seats in
the theatre. If it is less than 299 seats, his minimum salary will be $506
per week; if less than 399 seats, $580; if less than 449 seats, $773
(through June 30, 1988); and if less than 299 seats, $531 per week; if
less than 399 seats, $609; if less than 449 seats, $669; if less than 499
seats, $812 (through June 30, 1989); and if over 499 seats at the Broad-
way scale, which is $1,128 until December 31, 1988, and thereafter at
the rates agreed upon in the next negotiation. There are also payments
required for vacation (8 percent of salary), pension (8 percent of salary
and vacation), and an amount for welfare (hospitalization and medical
insurance, currently $77 per week). The press agent's weekly salary
begins no later than the day of the first rehearsal or four weeks before
the first performance. (If the show is transferring to Off-Broadway from
a showcase or from out of town, the producer can appeal to ATPAM
for a shorter period), whichever is earlier. ATPAM requires a two-week
bond (salary, vacation, pension, and welfare), plus $500 for expense
reimbursement.

ADVERTISING AGENCY

The press agent should be distinguished from the advertising agency. The advertising agency will handle the paid newspaper ads and other paid advertisements. The press agent is responsible for all of the publicity, but especially the publicity that is not paid for. The press agent will, of course, also assist the planning and execution of the paid advertising. Actually, the paid ads are usually prepared by the advertising agency after consultation with the producer, the press agent, and the general manager. There are a couple of advertising agencies in New York City that specialize in theatrical advertising, and they handle almost all of it. Your general manager or attorney will help you select one.

GENERAL MANAGER

Your production may have a general manager, a company manager, or both. If you are in an Off-Broadway theatre with under 200 seats, you must have a member of the Association of Theatrical Press Agents and Managers, commonly referred to as ATPAM, as either your press agent or your manager. If you are in an Off-Broadway theater with over 200 seats, then you must have both an ATPAM press agent and an ATPAM company manager.

The general manager will negotiate (in conjunction with the attorney), administer, and supervise the practical and financial procedures on behalf of the company, including all banking transactions. He will obtain, contact, and hire all required nonartistic theatre and production personnel that may become necessary; and, if requested by the producer, may also participate in the negotiation of contracts for the artistic personnel. He will, of course, prepare the production and operating budgets, as well as have the overall responsibility of the payment of all company bills from the company accounts, supervising the company accountant in the preparation and filing of all tax returns on time, and may even negotiate for the rental of the theatre. He will supervise the sale of all tickets and box office procedures and, in conjunction with the company's accounting firm, should render to the producer a weekly profit-and-loss statement of the company's operation, including an itemized accounting of all production expenditures. A good general manager is invaluable to an Off-Broadway production, especially when the producer lacks experience. The producer is, of course, responsible for the ultimate decisions of the producing company, but a good general manager will make it easier for the producer to make those decisions and will help put the decisions into effect.

COMPANY MANAGER

The duties of a general manager and a company manager may overlap, and there is sometimes not a clear delineation between the two jobs. Perhaps the most significant distinction is that the general manager's job is concerned with policy making and the company manager's job is on a nonpolicy-making level. The company manager attends to the actors' nonpersonal needs and is concerned with the day-to-day operation of the show on a business basis. ATPAM requires that the company manager he hired not later than the week in which the first rehearsal takes place or four weeks before the first performance (the producer may appeal to ATPAM for a shorter period if there is a good reason), whichever is earlier (and to be employed for one week following the close of the show), and the general manager will have been doing his job for *several* weeks before this. The company manager must be at the theatre each night to check the box office receipts, to count the house, to check the tickets, and to conduct whatever business is required at each performance.

The general manager who is a member of ATPAM may be his own company manager; however, more often than not, a general manager will employ another person to handle the chore of being the company manager. The minimum salary for an ATPAM company manager is the same as for press agents; based on the number of seats in the theatre. If it is less than 299 seats, it will be $506 per week; if less than 399 seats, $580; if less than 449 seats, $637; if less than 499 seats, $773, through June 30, 1988; and if less than 299 seats, $531 per week, if less than 399 seats, $609; if less than 449 seats, $669; if less than 499 seats, $812, through June 30, 1989; and if over 499 seats, at the Broadway scale, which is $1,128 until December 31, 1988, and thereafter at the rates agreed upon in the next negotiation. There are also payments required for vacation (8 percent of salary), pension (8 percent of salary and vacation), and an amount for welfare (hospitalization and medical insurance, currently $77 per week). ATPAM requires a two-week bond (salary, vacation, pension, and welfare) for the company manager.

ACCOUNTANTS AND ACCOUNTINGS

The New York Theatrical Financing Act enacted in 1964, which is part of the General Business Law of the State of New York, provides that every theatrical producer must, within four months after the end of each twelve month period (beginning with the first expenditure of investors' funds) or within four months after the last public performance of the original production in the state, whichever first occurs, furnish to all investors and to the Department of Law of the State of New York a written balance sheet and statement of profit and loss prepared by an independent public accountant, with an opinion by the accountant that these statements fairly present the financial position and results of operations of the production company. Each of these statements must be a "certified statement."

In addition, a producer must furnish each investor and the Department of Law of the state of New York with an accurate and truthful itemized statement of income and expenditures for every six-month period not covered by a previously issued certified statement which must be subscribed to by the producer as accurate, and must be furnished within three months after the close of such six-month period. After the last public performance in the state of the original production, the producer must report to the investors and to the Department of Law within four months after the end of each year thereafter with respect to subsequent earnings or expenditures by the production, which report must be subscribed by the producer as accurate.

The Department of Law of the state of New York is authorized to issue an exemption from furnishing certified statements if the offering is for less than $250,000 or if the offering is made to less than thirty-six persons.

In order to take advantage of this exemption, it is necessary that your attorney file a form known as an "Application for Exemption from Accounting Requirements—Article 26-A." This statement sets forth the fact that you are producing a play and that the total capitalization is in a specified amount and the number of persons to whom the offering has been made. The application will also state that the producer will see that the statements set forth above are prepared; however, they need not be certified statements. With each statement there must be a letter of transmittal stating that it constitutes a true, accurate, and complete reflection of the financial transactions of the production.

It is advisable that you select an accountant familiar with theatre, as the business problems of a theatrical production are somewhat unique. There are competent theatrical accountants in New York City who are conscious of all those peculiar problems that one may expect to encounter in an Off-Broadway show.

ATTORNEY

Hire a good theatrical attorney who knows the business. If he knows the business, you can rely on him to perform the kind of legal services you should have, and in addition, he will assist you with all kinds of advice that you, as a producer, will find helpful. If he knows the business, he won't charge you too much, because he will know that an Off-Broadway budget cannot compensate him for all the work he will do.

CHAPTER 7

Musicals

O FF-BROADWAY MUSICALS HAVE some additional items and additional personnel to consider. Musicals are of course more expensive to produce because arrangements are needed, musicians are needed, a choreographer and arranger must be hired. The consideration of selecting a theatre is different and of course casting is different. The actors must not only act well but must sing and move well. The original cast album can be very important to a musical.

A musical show may have an original story, may be an adaptation of a previously published novel or a previously published straight play, may be a revival, or may be a musical revue. At the present time, it is almost impossible to make it with a revue in a theatre as the theatre-going public during the past twenty-five years has been revued to death.

Off-Broadway revivals of shows previously produced on Broadway have currently been in vogue. The problem with such a revival is that most Broadway musicals have large casts and often in the transfer to Off-Broadway the show is not trimmed enough to sustain the play in such a small theatre with Off-Broadway ticket prices. Furthermore, what were successful Broadway productions of some years ago often cannot withstand the scaling down to the Off-Broadway level because the book was so flimsy in the first place. Musical theatre has undergone a development and evolution and the story in a musical of today has an importance that it did not have in the musicals of former years.

I have on many occasions spoken with producer clients and writer clients who are overwhelmed with the music for a particular play and, in fact, they are so overwhelmed that they cannot understand how the play can be anything but a smash hit with such music. "Just wait till you hear the music," is a common plea. What every producer doing a musical must always bear in mind is, how good is the book? It's rare that a musical in today's theatre is successful without a good book. In fact, many professional producers will not waste their time listening to the score of a musical until they have had a chance to read the script. If the script isn't strong, they feel that the music can't make any difference. Bear this in mind when you select a musical play for production. Excellent music will rarely make up for an almost-good script.

ORIGINAL CAST ALBUM

Usually the option agreement with the author, composer, and lyricist, will provide that the receipts from the original cast album will be shared with the author, composer, and lyricist receiving 60 percent of the net receipts and the producer receiving 40 percent of the net receipts. An original cast album differs from other subsidiary rights in that not only does the author, composer, and lyricist enter into the agreement, but the producer who controls the cast must also make the deal with the record company. The contract is often between the recording company and the producer, with the author, composer, and lyricist approving the contract, usually through their publishing company.

Usually the play must run for at least twenty-one performances before a recording company is obligated to make an original cast album. The contract will provide that the producer must furnish the cast, the members of the orchestra, and the conductor. The cast and musicians are actually paid by the recording company for their services; however, these payments will constitute an advance chargeable against the royalty payments paid to the author, composer, lyricist, and producer. In addition, the recording company will furnish the studio and all equipment. The producer has to furnish copies of the orchestrations and arrangements of the musical compositions.

Most often the agreement will provide that the recording company has an exclusive on an original cast album for a period of five years, and the performers are restricted for five years from performing for any other record company what they do on the original cast album. The royalty payable by the recording company to the author, composer, lyricist (it varies how they share this payment), and the producer, is usually between 5 and 10 percent of the suggested list retail price, or between 10 and 20 percent of the wholesale price. Royalties are almost always paid on 90 percent of the records sold. Very often there are provisions in the contract that the company need not pay royalties on free records, and will pay a greatly reduced royalty on records distributed through record clubs. One must be careful to limit in some fashion the number of free records and the distribution through record clubs at the reduced royalty, as it is possible for the record company to use your particular record as the advertising bait to sell other records.

Also bear in mind that the royalty payment is based on the replacement cost of the record (this is so whether it be based on a percentage of the wholesale or retail price), which means that they do not pay a royalty on the cost of the album cover, jacket, or box. Sometimes the cost of the album cover, jacket, or box is left for later determination. Sometimes the agreement fixes it in a given amount, and sometimes the agreement will provide that 10 percent of the wholesale price of the record will be deemed to be the cost of the cover. The contracts usually provide for billing credits to the recording company, an arbitration clause, and so on.

Of course, this is the barest outline of a contract for an original cast album, as there are many other important provisions in such an agreement. Even the terms that are herein mentioned are most negotiable, that is, they may vary in either direction from what is set forth above.

PUBLISHER

The publisher of the composer and lyricist is usually the one who arranges the original cast album, in exchange for which the publisher shares the composer-lyricist receipts from the album. When one thinks of a publisher, one usually thinks of publishing—that is, printing sheet music. This can be part of the job of a publisher; however, printing has become relatively less important. Most publishers are anxious to sign up a new composer and lyricist whom they consider talented, not for the right to print the sheet music that they write, but mostly because of the income that can flow from recordings, the manufacture of recordings and the performance of recordings.

MUSICIANS

There is no collective bargaining agreement with musicians for Off-Broadway. If all the musicians engaged for a show are nonunion, there is no union jurisdiction. However, if any musician engaged for a show is a member of any local of the American Federation of Musicians, then the producer must negotiate the minimum salary and any special conditions with Local 802 of the American Federation of Musicians, who have promulgated a Minimum Basic Agreement for Off-Broadway. The union takes the position that the minimum salaries for the musicians will depend on the location and the size of the theatre, and occasionally, also take into account the ticket price range, the total budget for the concessions given by other unions and other considerations. Since each show's conditions and requirements are different, you had best get some indication from your general manager as to what you may expect, either from past experience or from talking with other producers and general managers or from making a trip to the union office. Generally, the musician's base weekly salary ranges between $400 and $600 with the leader getting an additional one-half the base. Musicians playing more than one instrument receive additional payments for each additional instrument. If you are planning on using a synthesizer, or other electronic instruments, the union will require additional payments. As with other unions, there are vacation payments, pension and welfare payments, and a bond to be posted with the union representing one week's wages, vacation, pension and welfare.

ARRANGEMENTS AND MUSIC PREPARATION

When a composer finishes composing the music for a show, he has a lead sheet or at most an arrangement for the piano. Most Off-Broadway musicals have between two and five musicians and the music must be arranged for the various instruments that will be used. It goes without saying that you should not be extravagant with the number of musicians, as an Off-Broadway show cannot afford the luxury of a full pit orchestra. Some musicians double on one or more instruments. Many sax players can handle a clarinet, and this can mean dollar savings to you.

When a decision has been made as to the instruments that will be used, you will need an arranger to arrange the music for those instruments. Do not forget that, as the producer, the decision on the number of instruments is yours to make. Bear in mind that the composer and the director will be of invaluable service in assisting with this decision, but paying the bills is your job and not theirs. Use discretion consistent with your limited budget.

If you are going to employ union musicians, the union's promulgated Minimum Basic Agreement for Off-Broadway requires that "All orchestrations, copying and other musical preparation for the show shall be paid for according to the scales of the Local 802 General Price List for musical preparation . . ." and you will have to pay accordingly. As the union promulgates these rates and conditions, have your general manager assist you in estimating your costs. Rarely is union musical preparation less than $7,500 for a small Off-Broadway musical. If you are not going to employ union musicians, the musical arranger will usually be paid a fee based on a guarantee against a "per page charge" for the number of pages of music he delivers. The current range of the fees paid to nonunion musical arrangers is $2,500 to $5,000, including any necessary copying.

CHOREOGRAPHER

(See the section under "Director," in the previous chapter, for qualification of union jurisdiction) The choreographer will be engaged on a Society of Stage Directors and Choreographers contract and receive not less than the minimum required fee and advance required, which is 80 percent of the minimums for a director. With 50 percent being paid upon the signing of the contract, 25 percent being paid on the first day of rehearsal, and 25 percent being paid on the first day of the third week of rehearsal. In addition, the contract provides for a minimum royalty payment of 1½ percent of the gross weekly box office receipts.

MUSICAL DIRECTOR

The musical director is the conductor. He or she plays one of the instruments, almost always the piano; and is paid, as we noted, an amount as negotiated with the union. On occasions, the composer may insist on being the musical director.

CHAPTER 8

Rehearsals, Open, Run, or Close

S ELECTION OF A DATE for opening the show can be extremely important. Of course, the date for the commencement of rehearsals will
depend upon the date selected for the opening. If possible, you should
make every effort to open the show on a night when there is nothing
else opening. Your opening night date may be registered with the
League of Off-Broadway Theatres, and the first show registered for a
particular date would have priority as far as press coverage is concerned. It sometimes happens that a Broadway show is scheduled to
open on the same date on which an Off-Broadway show is scheduled.
Under such circumstances, even though the Broadway show may have
later decided on that date, the first string critics would give priority to
the Broadway show so it becomes necessary to change the Off-Broadway opening date.

There are certain times during the year that theatre business is
better than other times. Immediately after New Year's, there is a slack
period for several weeks. Religious holidays are generally slow nights.
Weekends of course are busier than weekdays. All of this should be
carefully considered so that you will have sufficient funds to withstand
the rough periods if your show is doing marginal business.

REHEARSALS

You will want to plan on at least three weeks of rehearsals; four weeks is not uncommon. As a producer, you should welcome the cast and staff at the first rehearsal. After the first rehearsal, you should make yourself somewhat scarce and should not interfere with the director's job. By this I mean that you should not spend every day during every rehearsal hour in the theatre with the director. It is important that you show your face backstage on occasion so that the cast and crew know you are interested in them and in the show. Of course, you should also follow the show's progress so that if the director is in trouble you may assist or replace him or her. This can be done without your constant presence in the theatre during rehearsals.

As the producer, you will have many other important things to do during rehearsal periods as there is a great deal of work that should be done in connection with the promotion of the play. During this period, you must complete the plans for your advertising campaign, arrange theatre parties, and set up every promotion device that you can conceive of. There will be tickets to order, programs to set up and get printed, posters to distribute. Your general manager will assist with these items. It is necessary to follow the progress of the play carefully. There will be rewriting sessions with the author, which you will want to attend. There will be personality problems with the cast that you will have to attend to. There will be hands to hold and tempers to cool. You will start losing all objectivity during this period if you are not careful— that is, if you still have any left.

PREVIEWS

Most Off-Broadway productions will preview for between seven and fourteen performances. To preview simply means that the show plays for paid audiences prior to the opening at a reduced ticket price. Previews serve the same purpose as out-of-town tryouts do for a Broadway show, to give the director, the cast, and all involved in the production an opportunity to see the audience reaction. Changes will be incorporated based on the audience response. Many Broadway shows have now abandoned the idea of out-of-town try-outs and use only previews. Both

Off-Broadway and Broadway shows sometimes get their pre-opening audience response by workshop or showcase productions, which are usually done by not-for-profit Off-Off-Broadway or resident theatres. Sometimes summer stock is the testing ground and sometimes it's the West End in London, England. It sometimes happens that some shows do better business during previews than they do after the reviews are published. This has led to the oft-repeated comment that "That show should have continued previewing and never should have opened."

During previews, producers will sometimes paper the house. The term *paper* is a name for free tickets. It may come as a surprise to you that people in the business usually pay for their tickets. The exceptions arise during previews or if the show is in trouble after opening. In both instances, an audience is desirable. A producer will generally call Actors' Equity and the USO to tell them that they may send some people to see the show free, or everyone in the cast and crew will be asked to call their friends and relatives to attend. In all events, it is terribly important that there be people watching the show, because an empty house can destroy the cast's morale. Papering for this reason should always be considered and used with discretion.

OPENING NIGHT

On opening night there is unbelievable excitement and much nervous tension in the air. Most shows open at 7:30 P.M., as the newspapers must make their deadline. The tickets may read 7:00 P.M. but it's usually 7:15 or 7:30 P.M. when the curtain goes up. You must make sure that it doesn't go up much later than 7:30 P.M., as you are certain to antagonize those reviewers who do have a deadline to make.

REVIEWS

The importance of reviews has not changed much in the last few years; however, the number of reviews in the City of New York by daily newspapers has markedly changed. At the present writing, the important dailies are the *New York Times,* the New York *Post,* and the *Daily News.* Of course, there are a host of other reviews that can be important, such as those in *New York, The New Yorker, Variety, The Village Voice,* and *Women's Wear Daily* (these are not necessarily in order of importance); however, it is pretty well believed that unless one gets a good review from the *New York Times* and at least one other daily, it's most difficult to keep the show running. The television reviews are becoming increasingly important, but we cannot minimize the extreme importance of the *New York Times.* I think that a *New York Times* rave review by itself might be enough without any of the other major reviews; however, it's most unlikely that a play that gets a good *New York Times* review won't get at least one other good review somewhere else.

Party

After the opening night performance, it is not uncommon for the producer or for the producing company to throw a cast party. It's usually labeled a "cast party," but the persons invited will include, in addition to the cast and crew, friends of the production and sometimes investors. The location of the party may vary, from someone's home (it should be large enough so that the cast and everyone else who's invited will not feel bashful about bringing guests with them) to a restaurant or hotel. I have attended Off-Broadway opening parties at some of the most exclusive restaurants in Manhattan, from Sardi's to One Fifth Avenue. Unfortunately, the degree of elegance of the party doesn't always reflect what happened on the stage. Some of the nicest parties have followed some of the most disappointing productions and vice versa. In all events, if the reviews are not good, the party will soon be over. The television reviews start coming around 11 P.M., and there may be three or fewer. The *New York Times* is out about 12:30 A.M., but usually the press agent gets the review around midnight from someone at the *Times.*

After Opening Night

After opening night, as the producer, you may be faced with a very serious decision—that is, whether or not you should close the show or attempt to run it. If the reviews are all bad, or mostly all bad, then your decision, although a heartbreaking one, is an easy one to make. You simply close the show as soon as possible. It will be difficult, but you should accept the facts of life. If you have rave reviews in all the dailies, again your decision is a relatively easy one. You've got to keep the show alive until the public starts buying tickets in large quantities, and you find yourself the producer of a sold-out show. With such reviews, this is not too difficult to contemplate.

The tough decision comes when you have one good review from the three dailies and some television support, or, later, some support from the weekly or monthly publications. Any situation that is less than all raves, where you figure that between 50 percent and 70 percent of the reviews are good, requires a most difficult business decision. Your objectivity at this particular moment may be rated as zero, but you must try to think realistically about what to do.

If you close the show immediately, you may be in a position to return to the backers some monies that will be left after paying off all of the obligations. Returning any money to backers is good public relations and you will be needing backers for later shows; that is, if you don't decide to give up show business forever. If you decide to run the show, you may obligate yourself for amounts in excess of the budget. It means that you, as the producer—the general partner—will have to reach into your pocket for the cash, as you are personally responsible for all sums spent in excess of the capitalization of the partnership. There, of course, may be some rich investors in the show who will help by making loans to the company that are returnable only from partnership profits, in an attempt to see that the play is kept alive until it has a reasonable chance for the word of mouth to start carrying the show. What's important is that a decision be made that has some basis in reality. It doesn't make too much difference whether you throw out your money or you throw out an investor's money, if in fact the money should not have been thrown out in the first place.

It is not unusual for a producer to request that persons receiving weekly royalties waive those royalties during losing weeks after opening if money is needed to keep the show alive. It is to the interest of everyone involved in the production that it get a long run, and such a request is not unreasonable, provided that, at the same time, the producer waives his producer's fee and, under some circumstances, even the cash office charge.

After the opening and the reviews are in, it's customary the following day to meet in the office of the advertising agency to put an ad

together. The pre-opening advertising budget for an Off-Broadway
show will range between $15,000 and $50,000. After the opening, the
reviews are carefully screened for "quotes," and a "quote" ad is often
put together. You can figure your advertising bill running between
$2,500 and $5,000, although sometimes it is even more than that.

It is permissable, without receiving permission, to quote an entire
review or part of a review, as long as you do not select bits and pieces
in such a manner as to misrepresent what was said. You cannot quote,
"A pretty awful play, and the parts were not well acted," as "A pretty
. . . play . . . well acted." If you try to distort the meaning, the
newspapers, most of the time, will not accept your ad, so it is not easy
for you to get yourself into trouble in this fashion even if you want to.

It is at this meeting at the ad agency that the very basic question,
to close or to try to run, must first be faced. A decision, of course, can
be postponed, but if it looks as if the chances of success are marginal,
then the decision ought not to be unreasonably delayed. At the meeting,
the general manager, the company manager, the press agent, the advertising agent, the attorney, the accountant, and any other interested
parties will attempt to counsel you. Please do not be upset if your
general manager, your accountant, your attorney, or other interested
parties who have had much theatre experience try to save you heart-
ache, wear and tear, and money by recommending that you close the
show. This does not mean that the persons making this recommenda-
tion like the show any less than they did before it opened, nor does it
mean that they like the show any less than you do. It just means that
they may have a more objective attitude about the possibility of making
a successful run of the show; they want to do the merciful thing and
save you as much time, energy, and money as can be saved with as little
hurt as possible.

I've seen it happen on many occasions that a general manager, or
one of the other interested parties, in all good conscience, recommends
that a show close and the producer, because of his fiery zeal, total
involvement, lack of sleep, and over-consumption of scotch, accuses the
well-intentioned manager of not having faith in the show and being a
quitter. This well-intentioned, totally correct, well-motivated adviser
will, of course, later be blamed by the producer for having been responsible for the failure of the show, simply because he wisely advised that
the show should be closed.

The decision to close the show, of course, in its final analysis, is the
producer's, and it's a terribly important decision. While making the

decision, please understand the motivation of the people around you. Know that they are trying to help you, to do what they can to assist you, and that this help should not be misunderstood to be traitorous or not in your best interest.

SCALING THE HOUSE, TWOFERS, DISCOUNT TICKETS

It may be very important to you how the house is scaled, which means what the ticket prices are. An off-Broadway musical customarily charges more than an Off-Broadway dramatic or comedy show. As you know, prices are higher on weekends. Your general manager will assist you in pricing the tickets so that you receive a maximum return on ticket sales and at the same time maintain attractive competitive prices.

"Twofers" are printed tickets that are distributed to be exchanged at the box office for two tickets for the price of one. These are printed and distributed throughout the city at hotels, schools, and other places of public assembly.

You may also purchase the use of a carefully selected list of 6,500 people that includes English teachers, drama teachers, speech teachers, literature and history teachers, principals, college educators, and high schools, junior high schools, and parochial schools, within a 125-mile radius of New York City. Such a mailing can be particularly useful if the play is one that would have appeal to students. The returns from this mailing list have proven very successful.

Twofers and student discount tickets would likely be used either at the beginning of a run or near the end of a run. Such tickets would be desirable at the inception if the show has a chance of running and it is necessary to stay alive for a few weeks until the tickets start selling. If your show didn't get decent reviews, don't think that twofers or student discount tickets can save the show. They may be very helpful in bridging a gap, but cannot alone make a financially successful show out of a flop. After the show has run for some length of time and business begins to fall off, you may also want to consider the use of twofers and student discount tickets.

MIDDLE THEATRES IN NEW YORK

Some mention should be made of "middle theatres." You will re-member that an Off-Broadway theatre is a theatre outside a certain geographical area in New York City, having more than 299 seats. However, there are some theatres that are neither Broadway theatres nor can they come within the definition of an Off-Broadway theatre as defined in the Actors' Equity Minimum Basic Contract, which is the commonly used definition. These theatres have acquired the name "middle theatres," and though the name seems to indicate that they are something between Broadway and Off-Broadway, the differences in the various theatres is sometimes great.

There are, for example, theatres outside the Broadway area contain-ing more than 299 seats. There also are theatres within the Broadway area containing 299 seats or less.

There is now another classification that technically comes within the definition of a Broadway theatre except that it contains a smaller number of seats than the usual Broadway theatre. There is a theatre within the Broadway area with fewer than 500 seats and most Broad-way theatres contain 900 seats or more. Even though the theatre is in the Broadway area, if it contains only 499 seats, it cannot and ought not to have the usual Broadway contract conditions as a theatre with 950 seats.

To confuse the situation even more, some theatres are not "theatres," in that they are operating under a cabaret license (which is different than a theatre license) and are considered "cabarets" rather than "theatres." Cabarets are supposed to serve drinks and food. What has happened is that they do not always do this, so that although the license is different, one would be hard-put sometimes to distinguish the difference between cabarets and theatres from one's observation of the premises.

The productions in middle theatres are eligible for "Tony" awards and the other benefits of a Broadway house. Each show in each type of theatre must negotiate separate union terms, which can vary. There are no fixed standard union contracts.

Before signing a lease or license agreement to go into a middle theatre, a producer would be wise to make certain that he understands all of the arrangements with various unions so that there is no question as to his obligations. Bear in mind that Actors' Equity is just one of the unions any new theatre must make its peace with. Since each theatre arrangement varies, it is impossible to delineate exactly what the union requirements are. Just make certain you know what you are getting yourself into.

CHAPTER 9

Repertories, Children's Theatre, and Off-Off-Broadway

REPERTORY COMPANY

E VERY NOW AND THEN someone gets the idea that there should be an Off-Broadway repertory company and proceeds to try to organize such a company, usually with a particular kind of theatre in mind. Of course, there is the Delacorte Theatre, where free productions of Shakespeare are presented in Central Park, which is geographically not Broadway, but technically this is not an Off-Broadway theatre because it seats over 300 persons. This is a completely different kind of an operation than most Off-Broadway producers will be engaged in since it receives grants and is not self-sustaining.

I have, on occasions, been confronted by a client who wants to set up a repertory theatre based on a particular ethnic origin, a particular author, or a special-interest kind of show—for example, suspense thrillers. If you want to organize a repertory company—that is, do more than one show with the same actors—you had best finance the production in such a way that you have enough money in advance to do three or four shows, without expecting enough remuneration from the first or second productions to do the third and fourth.

I've discovered from my clients' experience that it is usually easier to raise money for four separate shows, one at a time, than it is to raise enough money in the first instance to do four shows, one after the other. Someone will always find a reason why they like one show or two shows but not all of them. Most people are not really anxious to get involved in a producing company that will go on producing indefinitely, keeping all of the money that it earns to do more shows rather than returning the money to the investors. Even if the company makes money on the first or second show, if a repertory company runs long enough, it will continue to produce shows until it eventually runs out of money. It is highly unlikely that the company can continually come in with successes, and by the law of averages, the money must eventually run out.

With one show, the investors know that after the reserve is raised, all of the net profits will be paid to them. With a repertory company, the investors know that after the first show the profits will be kept for the next show. Even where the partnership is formed for the production of one single play, the limited partnership agreement, as we earlier learned, may provide that the profits may be used for additional productions of this particular play, so it is possible that the investors will be investing their money in future productions of the same play. At least the investors know what they are getting into when they invest in a single play, and know that they are fastening their faith to this single, known play.

Children's Theatre

Most usually, the groups that produce children's theatre are repertory companies; the same actors and actresses present different children's plays. Some of the children's theatre that I represent is not just attractive to children but has remarkable appeal for adults.

If you are contemplating producing children's theatre, you should be aware of the fact that there are serious business problems that are very nearly insurmountable. The artistic problems are solvable; that is, reasonable compromises can be made. Most of the children's shows are presented on Saturday morning in a theatre that already has another production in it. As a result, it is often necessary to improvise easily movable sets and props and to present the show on a stage already filled with the sets that are there for the show that is presently occupying the theatre. The lights are all focused for the play that is in the theatre and cannot be changed. This kind of an adjustment may be slightly inconvenient but can easily be made.

The business problems with the production of children's theatre can readily be seen when one realizes that the shows play to a relatively poor market. Children cannot afford to pay and their parents won't pay what is charged for tickets to an adult show. You must pay the needed box office help, ushers, stage manager, and so on, and it's easy to see that the chance of making money from Off-Broadway children's theatre is possible but not probable. You would have to cut corners and fill, or nearly fill, the theatre for every performance—or be heavily endowed.

There are many theatres outside the City of New York that will seat 600, 800, or 1,000 children, and even larger tents that offer a potential for the presentation of children's theatre. The problem is to make certain that there are enough bookings in such places to pay for all of the expenses incidental to running a going business.

OFF-OFF-BROADWAY

One must not overlook the contribution that has been made to theatre by what is known as the Off-Off-Broadway theatres. The Off-Off-Broadway theatres, if they are functioning with Equity actors, present shows either as a showcase or as a workshop production. There are specific regulations promulgated by Actors' Equity Association, setting forth the requirements of a showcase presentation and a workshop presentation, and members of Actors' Equity are forbidden to work in a production unless there is strict compliance with the rules as established by Equity. The reason, of course, is to make certain that actors are not exploited.

What very often happens, and everyone in the business knows that it's happening, is that an Off-Off-Broadway producer purports to have a non-Equity production and does not comply with the Equity regulations. Oftentimes, Equity actors who are unemployed are so anxious to be working that they will appear in an Off-Off-Broadway non-Equity production under an assumed name. This kind of dishonesty is also not recommended. There's no good reason why a producer ought to jeopardize the career of an actor by asking that actor to do something contrary to the regulations of the Association. Either present a non-Equity production or abide by the rules of Actors' Equity Association. It means fewer headaches, and if you are going to be in the business, it's desirable that you establish yourself as one who is responsible and honest.

At the time this is being written, there are, in Manhattan alone, over one hundred and twenty-five Off-Off-Broadway theatres in existence. Sixty-five of these theatres are members of the Off-Off-Broadway Alliance, a cooperative organization that was established to promote recognition for Off-Off-Broadway as a significant cultural force and to help its member theatres achieve their artistic goals.

At any particular time, it is possible to see a variety of different productions, which includes plays from great classical theatre as well as new original works. The only identifying feature that distinguishes Off-Off-Broadway from Off-Broadway is the fact that almost all Off-Off-Broadway theatres are not-for-profit theatres (as opposed to the Off-Broadway commercial theatre). This means that they are financed by gifts, contributions, and grants. Off-Broadway theatre, as we know, is in the business of making money and is financed by investments.

Most Off-Off-Broadway theatres operate on annual budgets that range from $30,000 to over $500,000 annually. Yes, there is this huge disparity. The middle-range annual budget (if there is such a thing, which there probably isn't) would probably be between $150,000 and $200,000.

The average production budget for a particular show is probably $50,000 to $150,000. Of course, some shows are produced for less. The average production budget (if they worked it out) for a particular show in most of the theatres with large annual budgets would be in the neighborhood of $100,000.

There has recently been a great deal of publicity about negotiations between a committee representing Off-Off-Broadway and Actors' Equity Association. The conflict stems from the economic facts of Off-Off-Broadway life—namely that, in order to subsist, the Off-Off-Broadway theatres cannot pay the actors anything substantial. At the same time, Actors' Equity Association would like to know that if something good happens as a result of the original Off-Off-Broadway production, the original actors will be part of the new production or compensated in some manner. Of course, if the union demands become enough, the new commercial producer who wants to convert the Off-Off-Broadway show to a Broadway or Off-Broadway production, faced with having to use actors he does not want, or paying them an excessive amount of money for the privilege of not using them, may simply walk away from the project. This could hurt the author of the play and could also hurt the Off-Off-Broadway theatre that will share in some of the proceeds from the commercial production, usually to the extent of 1 percent to 5 percent of the net profits.

The dispute has centered around how much the cast can be paid, whether admission can be charged for the production, whether advertising may be done, how many performances may be presented under the code, and the like.

The dispute continues, but in the meantime, the Off-Off-Broadway theatres are operating under the showcase code, often with the pilot project rider. The committee has come forth with a specific proposal and perhaps in the future there may be some modifications of the existing code.

Most Off-Off-Broadway theatres are not-for-profit corporations and, as I have stated, have an annual budget rather than a per-show budget. Since they consider themselves the best theatre laboratory in the world, in many instances the nonsuccesses of Off-Off-Broadway are as important to the theatre as the successes.

CHAPTER 10

Vitally Important Odds and Ends

THE ART OF NEGOTIATION

A BRIEF WORD OR TWO is in order at this time on the art of negotiation. One must always be conscious of the fact that there are many factors working at the same time and that the contracts discussed in this book are not negotiated in a vacuum. Every item requested by either side can affect the other items that will end up in the agreement, in that there is a good deal of give and take, changing, exchanging, and bartering within certain defined limits. I know that someone will, for example, insist that they know a producer who obtained an option for an advance payment of less than $100. Of course, there *are* times when options are acquired for the payment of only a dollar. Just as someone will surely tell me that in some instances producers will only have to pay a royalty of 4 percent of the gross weekly box office receipts, or in another instance, must pay 10 percent of the gross weekly box office receipts.

I have already noted that the rare or unusual is not within the purview of this book. The give and take, change and exchange, that takes place is predicated on the parties playing the game in the same ball park. If one party comes to the negotiations making an extreme demand, outside the normal limits, the negotiations may be over before they start. It is not a good negotiation tactic to make unreasonable demands. If the offer is not within reason, the other party will not bid against it.

In this business, when one is not totally aware of all of the ramifications of the contractual arrangements, it's fairly easy to become alarmed about percentage arrangements. In order to get a particular performer, for instance, who can enhance the production to come with the show, and who otherwise would not, I have at times recommended to a producer client to make an assignment of a part of the producer's profits to the person. That performer may be the one who makes a difference between a successful show and a flop. On such occasions, I am often confronted with the comment that other producers never give anything away.

On other occasions, I've been told, "Why should I pay eight percent to the author when an author in most agreements only gets five or six percent?" There are times when one must not be fenced in by the kind of percentage arrangements that have been previously made. It is a basic axiom, and one that I repeat time and again to every client I have ever represented in theatre, that 2 percent of something can be a tremendous amount of money, and 90 percent of nothing is nothing. What I'm saying, in effect, is that the percentage amount is not as important as what you are taking the percentage of. A producer who starts with 50 percent of the profits of the show, even if he had to give away as much as 30 percent to the people who are responsible for making it a smash hit, would still do very nicely even if he ultimately ended up with only 20 percent of the profits. On the other hand, if the show doesn't make it, a producer who doesn't give away any of his profits but retains all 50 percent ends up with 50 percent of nothing.

I'm not suggesting that a producer ought to go around needlessly giving away percentages of the producer's profits, nor am I suggesting that an author should be paid a larger percentage than is necessary to acquire the property. Giving does not ensure a success, but not getting the right people because one won't give may mean failure. What I am suggesting also is that the numerical percentage amount is something that shouldn't be frightening to a producer. What one is receiving in exchange for the percentage amount, and the importance of the contribution to the production, is the important consideration.

It sometimes happens that an author or a director will come to the negotiations not represented by an attorney or an agent. Whenever I am the attorney representing the producer and negotiate with another party who is not represented by someone who knows the business, I deal with the nonrepresented person on a different level. If I negotiate a contract on behalf of a producer, and the author is represented by an agent or an attorney, then under such circumstances I get as much for my client as I am capable of convincing the other party I should get. When I deal with someone who is not represented by an attorney or agent, I am inclined to lean over backward to make certain that that person is treated fairly.

What can happen and sometimes does happen is that I will deal with someone on behalf of a producer, with an author for example, who is not represented by a party who is knowledgeable in the business. I arrange what I deem to be a most fair option contract. When the contract is completed but not yet signed, the author, not really understanding how fair the contract is, may give second thoughts to the arrangement and decide to consult an agent or an attorney. The next thing I know, I get a telephone call and someone is telling me that he now represents the author and he wants to start the negotiations on the contract.

This is an unfair way of doing business, because he would like me now to negotiate against the contract I, myself, prepared and agreed to in an attempt to be fair when the author had no counsel. If I had been negotiating against someone who did know the business, I would have taken a much firmer position from the beginning. For me to start negotiating with someone when the basis for the negotiations is to be a contract that I have already established as fair is an unreasonable imposition upon me and my client. Under such circumstances, I have to insist upon remaining firm and taking the position that there is nothing further to talk about and nothing to negotiate, except perhaps some very minor points that might possibly have been overlooked.

Perhaps the most important thing that one must know before one can effectively and intelligently negotiate contracts dealing with theatre is to know what items are important and what are not, as well as the degree of importance of each particular item. The real difference between someone who negotiates well and someone who does not rests in the ability to give in on the items that are not really important and to hold out and stand firm for those things that are. People who are not theatre-oriented rarely know what is important to negotiate for. One acquires this knowledge through experience.

CONFLICTS OF INTEREST

It sometimes happens that a producer produces a show in order to direct the show or act in it, or a producer produces a show that he or she has authored. One must always be especially careful of such an arrangement.

In the first place, there will be a conflict of interest when you, as the author, sell yourself, as the producer, the rights to produce the play. Under such circumstances, when I represent an author-producer, I make certain that the producer gets the best possible deal. The reason I do this is that the producer will raise money from investors who I feel need representation. So, in a sense, I look out for the investors' interests. What an author-producer does as producer affects others (the investors), and what he does as the author affects only himself. Since the producer is dealing with himself, he must do as much or more than another author would do for the producing company in the terms of the option agreement granting the rights. If the producer were negotiating at arm's length with another author, there would be no question but that the producing company would end up with everything it could get and should have. There's always a question when one deals with oneself. Therefore, I make the party lean over backward, under such circumstances, in order to be fair.

In the second place, if the producer is the director, how does he fire himself if he isn't doing a good job of directing if he is also the boss? There's always this danger when a producer directs his own production. Furthermore, the play can become very one-dimensional if the producer is the director. There's something to be said for a different point of view judging the director's work. When someone tries to wear too many hats, it's very easy to lose perspective. If there is more than one producer, and if one of the producers is the director, the one who is not directing must always be in a position to replace the producer-director if things are not going well. A provision to this effect should always be incorporated into the joint venture agreement.

It is not unusual for an actor to assume a different name if he is acting in a show in which he is one of the producers. In doing so, the actor admits that he is doing something that he does not want publicized. There is a feeling that it does not look good for an actor to have to produce the show to get the job.

There are drawbacks to a producer hiring himself as an actor, for the producer ought always to be in a position to replace even the star of the show if things are not going as they should.

Obviously, there are some striking exceptions that may be called to my attention. There are indeed several famous names in the theatre (Sir Laurence Olivier, Orson Welles, Eva Le Gallienne) who were competent as actors, directors, and producers, and on occasions performed all three roles at the same time. It's just not usual nor advisable. Most of us will do well if we can handle any one of these three jobs in a competent, professional way.

PACKAGE DEALS

You should also be very skeptical of any "package deal" that may be offered to you. It sometimes happens that, for whatever reason, someone wants to sponsor a particular person and offers you a property if you use a particular person as the director. You may on the other hand be offered all or a large part of the financing if you use a particular actress. There is nothing wrong with one of the people you cast bringing in a sum of money, but if the reason for the casting is the money, then you are making a mistake. As a producer, you must never abdicate your responsibility of selecting the best people for the right reasons. To do a play badly simply because it was easier to get the money that way will not only mean a great waste of your time and energy but will contribute to a reputation for expedience rather than judgment and taste.

THE LEAGUE OF OFF-BROADWAY THEATRES AND PRODUCERS

A most appropriate and useful way in which an industry may solve its problems is the formation of a group in which persons and businesses connected with that industry meet to discuss their common problems and to find a way to solve them by frank and open discussions. Such is the case of the League of Off-Broadway Theatres and Producers. Twenty-eight years ago, the League was formed by the theatre owners and producers operating Off-Broadway to perpetuate the Off-Broadway theatre. They joined together to resolve the common problems that had been confronting them. The League of Off-Broadway Theatres and Producers, through the years, has established a labor relationship with Actors' Equity Association, the Association of Theatrical Press Agents and Managers (ATPAM), and the Society of Stage Directors and Choreographers (S.S.D.C.), in which the parties have negotiated employment contracts covering the Off-Broadway theatre. In addition, the League serves as an information conduit regarding activities that take place, and registers the dates of opening night performances so that there are no conflicts among the Off-Broadway theatres. It is most advisable that a producer who is seriously interested in producing Off-Broadway become a member of this organization. Membership information may be had by telephoning the office of the secretary-treasurer of the League, who is currently George Elmer, at telephone number (212) 730-7130.

ETHICS—HONESTY

It's not just a matter of ethics, but honesty is good business. Bear this in mind in all of your theatrical dealings.

It sometimes happens that someone who is producing an Off-Broadway show gets the mistaken idea that he or she can accomplish certain things by being devious. Sometimes the fervor to do a show becomes so great that one is willing to cut corners and do things that one would otherwise not think of doing. It's true that "the show must go on," but it must go on right. I have on occasion had clients try to use me in their devious dishonest maneuvers. For an example, there have been occasions when someone will negotiate for something they do not have the money to pay for, and will try to impose upon me to call the other party to tell them that I'm holding the money. Of course, if I'm not going to be dishonest myself, and I'm not, then I'm not going to permit a client to use me to assist in his dishonesty. If you haven't raised all of the money necessary to release the funds to you to start the show, then don't start using the money and don't start the show. It's not only dishonest, it's bad business. Don't misrepresent to someone that you've signed the star unless you have signed that star. It's not only dishonest, it's bad business. Don't misrepresent by saying that you've raised $150,000 of the budget if you have only raised $50,000. *It's not only dishonest, it's bad business.*

You must know, of course, that you are going into a very risky business. When the chance of a successful Off-Broadway production is something like one out of twelve, you realize that the odds are against you. Even that one out of twelve that is successful may not prove to be the kind of smash hit that will return tremendous amounts of money to you. There are all kinds of reasons for wanting to produce a show, and chances are that the money is not the sole motivation. If it is, then it would be easier to find other businesses with a greater chance of success.

The theatre business is a small family. If you are serious about becoming a producer, then you are not in the business to simply get one show produced, but intend to produce other shows. Your reputation will follow you in everything you do. You will be known in this little family for what you really are. It's just as easy, if not easier, to be honest in your dealings, not just because it's ethical, but because it's good business. I know the "successful" producers in the business who are not honest. Everyone in the business knows them. They are not successful because of their dishonesty. They are not respected, they are not appreciated, they are not good businessmen. Play square, not just because it's the right thing to do, but also because it's good business.

I'm often asked, "Aren't theatre people immoral or dishonest?" This question of course is utter nonsense. Theatre people are moral and immoral, honest and dishonest, just like other people. The difference is that theatre people have different problems. Of course, the implication is that all people have problems. For the most part, my friends and clients in theatre are considerate, intelligent, bright, and sensitive people.

GOOD PRODUCING

A show, more than almost any other business, is a team project. Until you've been in the business and have seen how things happen, it's hard to understand that everything and everyone is dependent on everyone else in the production. Of course, when the actors are on stage, they influence each other, but I am talking about something more than that. There's an interaction between the actors and the stage manager, between the director and the actors, between the actors and the company manager, between the stage manager and the producer, between the producer and the general manager, between the attorney and the producer, between the press agent and the actors, and so on.

If you have a successful production, as the producer, don't break your arm patting your back, because you didn't do it by yourself. Probably the one thing that you did that you want to take the least credit for, but that may have contributed the most to the show, is that you have selected very good people for each of the areas of endeavor and turned over the reins to them. A good producer doesn't have to be a person who does, or even knows, how to do all of the jobs in a production. A good producer can be a person who knows how to select all of the people who will do these jobs in a remarkable fashion; and, in selecting the people, to select those whose chemistry works together, who vibrate on the same wavelength, and who together make magic. When that marvelous, spellbinding thing happens, and everything seems to fall into place and work, you will wake up one morning and have a hit on your hands.

APPENDICES

Option Agreement

This AGREEMENT is made and entered into as of the 1st day of March, 1989, by and between Rich Rich whose address is 987 W. 65 Street, New York, New York 98765, and Rob Rob whose address is 654 E. 32 Street, New York, New York, 43210 ("Producers") and Sandra Sand whose address is 444 S. 55 Street, Brooklyn, New York, 34343 ("Author").

WITNESSETH:

WHEREAS, Author has written and composed the book, music and lyrics for a musical play presently entitled "Mink" (the "Play"); and

WHEREAS, Producers desire to produce the Play and to acquire Author's services in connection therewith; and

NOW, THEREFORE, in consideration of the mutual promises and covenants herein contained, and other good and valuable consideration, it is agreed:

1. <u>Representations and Warranties</u>

Author represents, warrants and guarantees that:

(a) Author is the sole Author of the Play and that the same is original with such Author except to the extent that it contains material which is in the public domain and was not copied in whole or in part from any other work, nor will the uses contemplated herein violate, conflict with or infringe upon the copyright, right of publicity or any other right of any person, firm or corporation; and

(b) Author has not granted, assigned, encumbered or otherwise disposed of any right, title or interest in or to the Play or any of the rights granted hereunder. Author has the sole and exclusive right to enter into this Agreement and the full warrant and authority to grant the rights granted hereby.

(c) There is not now outstanding and there has not been any grant, assignment, encumbrance, claim, contract, license commitment or other disposition of any right, title, or interest in or to the Play or any of the rights granted hereunder to Producers or by which the exploitation of the rights granted to Producers and the enjoyment and exercise thereof by Producers might be diminished, encumbered, impaired, invalidated or affected in any way.

2. Indemnity

(a) Author will indemnify Producers against any and all losses, costs, expenses including reasonable attorneys fees, damages or recoveries (including payments made in settlement, but only if Author consents thereto in writing) caused by or arising out of the breach of the representations or warranties herein made by Author.

(b) Producers agree that they will be solely liable for all costs incurred in connection with any presentation of the Play and they shall indemnify and hold Author harmless from any claims arising therefrom.

3. Grant of Rights and Author's Services

Author has delivered a complete draft of the Play to Producers and Author hereby agrees:

(a) In consideration of the sum of $400.00 as an advance against the royalty payments hereinafter provided, the Author hereby grants to the Producers the sole and exclusive right and license to produce the Play and to present it as a professional Off-Broadway or middle theatre production (and a developmental production) in the City of New York to open on or before March 1, 1990. If before March 1, 1990, the Producers give Author notice, together with payment of $400.00, the right and license herein granted shall be extended for the play to open on or before March 1, 1991.

(b) That she will perform such services as may be reasonably necessary in making revisions;

(c) That she will assist in the selection of the cast and consult with, assist and advise director, scenic, lighting and costume designers in the problems arising out of the production;

(d) That she will attend rehearsals of the Play as well as out of town performances (if any) prior to the New York Opening of the Play.

4. Outside Production Date

Although nothing herein shall be deemed to obligate Producers to produce the Play, Producers shall without limitation as to any other rights which may be granted hereunder, have the option to produce the Play as an off-off-Broadway or regional theatre production or a workshop or showcase presentation at any time prior to the Off-Broadway or middle theatre production. Unless on or before March 1, 1990 (or March 1, 1991, if the option is extended), Producers produce and present the Play on the speaking stage in a regular evening bill as a paid public performance in an Off-Broadway or middle theatre in New York City, Producers' right to produce the Play and to the services of Author shall then terminate.

5. Exclusivity and Continuous Run

The rights granted to the Producers are the sole and exclusive rights to produce the Play (the Producers may acquire an option pursuant to the terms of this agreement as hereinafter set forth to produce the Play in the British Isles and in the U.S. and Canada and on tour), and the author agrees that she will not grant the rights to permit anyone to perform the said Play in any media (exclusive of movies) within the United States of America, Canada or the British Isles, during the term of the option herein granted and the run of the Play, or during the period that the Producers retain any rights or option to produce the Play anywhere in the United States, Canada or the British Isles, and further agrees that she will not grant the right to anyone to do a movie version of the Play which would be released during the term of the option or the run of the Play, or during the period that the Producers retain any right or option to produce the Play in the United States,

Canada or the British Isles, without the written consent of the Producers, which consent will not be unreasonably withheld.

If the Play is produced within the option period herein granted, the exclusive right to produce the Play in New York City shall continue during its New York City continuous run. The Play shall be deemed closed (that is, the New York City continuous run shall have terminated) if no paid performances have been given in New York City for a period of four (4) weeks. After the Play has closed and after all options to produce the Play have expired, all rights shall revert to the Author subject to any other terms specifically herein set forth.

If the Play is produced outside the City of New York on tour or otherwise, the exclusive right to produce the Play after the option period herein stated shall continue during its outside New York City continuous run. Outside New York City continuous run as herein defined shall mean that there shall not be a lapse of more than eight (8) weeks between presentations of the Play before a paying audience. If the option period has expired and if more than eight (8) weeks elapse between any such paid performances, then all rights shall revert to the author except those that may have been specifically herein vested.

6. Consideration

(a) In consideration of the foregoing, and of Author's services in writing and revising the Play and Author's agreement to perform services in connection with the production of the Play as herein provided, Producers agree to pay Author such sums as may equal five percent (5%), (going to six and one-half percent (6½%) on recoupment of the total production costs), of the gross weekly box office receipts of each production of the Play produced under Producers' management, license or control.

(b) Anything to the contrary herein notwithstanding if all other royalty participants, including the Producers, with respect to the Producers' fee, agree to a waiver of one-half of their usual royalty, the Author agrees to waive one-half of her royalty, that is two and one-half percent of the gross weekly box office receipts, until recoupment of the total production costs of the production (less bonds, deposits and other recoverable items) on the express condition that 1.) Each week's operating profits are paid directly to the investors as payment toward recoupment of such total production costs; and 2.) After recoupment of such total production costs the Author's royalty shall be in an amount equal to seven percent (7%) of the gross weekly box office receipts. Producers do hereby agree to such waiver of one-half of Producers' fee.

(c) If the Play is presented for a workshop or showcase production or in a regional or off-off-Broadway theatre Author will be paid a fee of $25.00 per performance.

The Author shall be entitled to inspect the books and records of the Producers for any production hereunder during regular business hours and upon reasonable notice, but not more often than once every six months.

7. Traveling Expenses and Per Diem

Author shall have the right to be present at any or all out of town performances of the Play up to the official New York Opening. The hotel and traveling expenses to be paid by Producers to Author in connection with such out of town performances of the Play, if any, shall be (i) $100 per day for hotel and/or other living expenses and (ii) economy air transportation expenses to and from Author's places of residence as indicated herein, and from place to place out of town.

8. Tours and Out of Town Productions

Producers' production rights hereunder shall be deemed to include "bus and truck" tours of the Play and other out of town (outside of New York City) productions of the Play (whether first class or Off-Broadway type productions) provided Producers have presented the Play hereunder for not fewer than twenty-one paid public performances. For each out of town other than first class production, Author will receive three (3) months' notice from the last paid public performance and a fee of five hundred dollars ($500) to be paid as an advance against royalties in the amount as set forth in paragraph 6 (a) above. In connection with any such engagements, Author's royalties may be computed on the basis of Producers' receipts (including but not limited to fixed fees, guarantees, profits, rentals, and any Producers' share of box office receipts), but only if the following conditions exist in connection with such engagements or productions:

(i) that Producers' gross compensation, whether direct or indirect, for presenting the production is a fixed fee or a combination of a guarantee and a share of the box office receipts, payable to the Producers by a so-called "local promoter" or "local sponsor" or other third party acting in a similar capacity; and

(ii) that all other creative royalty participants' royalties and the Producers' management fee be computed on the same basis.

If the foregoing conditions in subdivisions (i) and (ii) hereof are not met, Author's royalties shall be computed on the gross box office receipts of any such engagements and productions.

It is understood that Producers shall have the right to present first class out of town productions whether or not Producers have exercised the Broadway option under paragraph 10 and that such performances shall be governed by the terms of the Dramatists Guild, Inc., Approved Production Contract ("APC") as herein set forth in paragraph 10 of this Agreement provided, however, that the terms of this paragraph shall also be applicable.

9. Production in the United Kingdom and Ireland

If the Producers have produced the Play Off-Broadway or in a middle theatre in New York for not less than twenty-one paid public performances, Producers shall have the exclusive right to produce the Play on the speaking stage in the United Kingdom and in Ireland upon all the terms and conditions which apply to a New York production, to open at any time up to and including six (6) months after the close of the production in New York, upon sending Author written notice within two months from the close of the last paid public performance accompanied by a payment of one thousand dollars ($1,000) as a non-returnable advance against the royalties in an amount as set forth in paragraph 6 (a) above. Producers may produce the Play in association with or under lease to a British or Irish producer. In such case Producers' obligation to make the royalty payments herein provided shall remain unimpaired. If it is to be produced on the West End in London, such contract between Producers and the British or Irish Producers shall require the Play to be produced under the same terms as would apply if the original New York production had been produced under the Approved Production Contract for a first class production.

10. Broadway Production

Producers shall have the exclusive option, exercisable by written notice given to Author at any time prior to the later of (i) the expiration of the Outside Production Date described in paragraph 4 hereof if there is no Off-Broadway or middle theatre production of the Play, or (ii) sixty (60) days after the last performance of the Play Off-Broadway or in a middle theatre, to acquire the right to present the Play as a first class production on Broadway in New York City. The time within which the foregoing option may be exercised shall be automatically extended if Producers acquire or exercise rights to produce and present the Play on tour or in the United Kingdom and Ireland under paragraphs 8 or 9 hereof, and Producers may then exercise such option at any time prior to sixty days (60) after the last performances of a British or Irish production, tour or other out of town performance under paragraphs 8 and 9 hereof.

In the event Producers elect to present the play on Broadway and exercise the option under paragraph 10 (a) hereof, the minimum terms of the Approved Production Contract then in use shall become applicable and shall govern the relationship between Author and Producers with respect to the first class presentation in the United States and/or Canada, and the exploitation of other rights under the Contract.

If prior to the Broadway Opening, Producers have become entitled to a share of subsidiary rights in the Play pursuant to this Agreement, such Broadway production shall not affect, limit or reduce such Producers' share thereof and Producers shall continue to be entitled to receive such share irrespective of the number of Broadway performances of the Play and irrespective of anything contained in the Approved Production Contract to the contrary, provided that if Producers become entitled to a greater share of subsidiary rights pursuant to the Approved Production Contract, Producers shall receive such greater share, but not shares from both contracts.

In the event Producers shall elect to exercise the option in accordance with paragraph 10 (a) hereof, then Author shall enter into and execute and deliver the Approved Production Contract within seven (7) days of Producers' submission thereof to Author. Notwithstanding the failure or omission of Author to execute and/or deliver the said Contract, it is agreed that upon exercise of such option, all rights in and to the Play which are granted and transferred to Producers by Author in accordance with the said Contract shall be deemed automatically vested in Producers effective as of the date of the exercise of the option, which rights shall be irrevocable under any and all circumstances except in accordance with the terms of the Approved Production Contract.

11. Force Majeure

If Producers shall be prevented from exercising any option hereunder, or if any production of the Play hereunder shall be prevented or interrupted, due to epidemic, fire, action of the elements, strikes, labor disputes, governmental order, court order, act of God, public enemy, wars, riots, civil commotion, illness or any other similar cause beyond the Producers' control, whether of a similar or dissimilar nature, such prevention or interruption shall not be deemed a breach of this agreement or a cause for forfeiture of Producers' rights hereunder, and the time for exercise of such option and/or the time by which the first paid public performance must take place shall be extended for the number of days during which the exercise of such option or presentation of such production was prevented; provided that if a failure to exercise any option or any prevention or interruption of production due to any such cause shall continue for sixty (60) days, then Author shall have the right to terminate Producers' production rights for the interrupted run or terminate Producers' right to exercise such option (as the case may be) by written notice to Producers.

12. Approvals and Changes

(a) No changes in the text of the Play shall be made without approval of Author. Such changes shall become the property of Author. Cast, director, scenery, costume and lighting designers, and permanent replacements thereof of all productions of the Play hereunder shall be subject to Author's approval not to be unreasonably withheld. The Author does hereby specifically approve John Jones as the director of any productions of the Play in any media.

(b) In any case where Producers request the approval of Author as provided above and the Producers are unable to obtain Author's response to such request forty-eight hours after having sent him a telegram requesting the same, or personally requesting the same, then Author's consent and/or approval shall be deemed to have been given. Author shall have the right to appoint in writing a representative to respond to requests for approval.

13. Subsidiary Rights

Although the Producers are acquiring the rights and services of the Author solely in connection with the production of the Play, the Author recognizes that by a successful production the Producers make a contribution to the value of the uses of the Play in other media. Therefore, although the relationship between the parties is limited to play production as herein provided, and the Author owns and controls the Play with respect to all other uses, nevertheless, if the Producers have produced the Play as provided herein the Author agrees that the Producers shall receive an amount equal to the percentage of net receipts (regardless of when paid) specified hereinbelow received by Author if the Play has been produced for the number of consecutive performances set forth and if before the expiration of ten (10) years subsequent to the date of the last paid public performance of the Play in New York City, any of the following rights are disposed of anywhere throughout the world: motion picture, or with respect to the Continental United States and Canada, any of the following rights: radio, television, touring performances, stock performances, Broadway performances, Off-Broadway performances, amateur performances, foreign language performances, condensed tabloid versions, so-called concert tour versions, commercial and merchandising uses, and audio and video cassettes and discs: Ten percent (10%) if the Play shall run for at least twenty-one (21) consecutive paid performances; twenty percent (20%) if the Play shall run for at least forty-two consecutive paid performances; thirty percent (30%) if the Play shall run for at least fifty-six (56) consecutive paid performances; forty percent (40%) if the Play shall run for sixty-five (65) consecutive paid performances or more. For the purposes of computing the number of performances, provided the Play officially opens in New York City, the first paid performance shall be deemed to be the first performance, however only seven paid previews will be counted in this computation.

14. Computation of Royalties

"Gross weekly box office receipts" shall be computed in the manner determined by the League of New York Theatres and Producers provided, however, that in making such computation there shall be deducted: (a) any Federal admission taxes; (b) any commissions paid in connection with theatre parties or benefits; (c) those sums equivalent to the former five (5%) percent New York City Amusement Tax, the net proceeds of which are set aside in Pension and Welfare Funds in the theatrical unions and ultimately paid to said funds; (d) commissions paid in connection with automated ticket distribution or remote box offices, e.g., Ticketron (but not ticket brokers) and any fees paid or discounts allowed in connection with credit card sales; (e) subscription fees; and (f) discounts provided to any discount ticket service (e.g. TDF).

15.   Accounting

Within seven (7) days after the end of each calendar week Producers agree to forward to Author the amounts due as compensation for such week and also, within such time, to furnish office statements of each performance of the Play during such week, signed by the treasurer or treasurers of the theatre in which performances are given, and counter-signed by Producers or their duly authorized representative. Box office statements and payments due for productions presented more than 500 miles from New York City may be furnished and paid within fourteen (14) days after the end of each week, and for productions presented in the United Kingdom or Ireland, within forty-five (45) days. In cases where Author's compensation depends on operating profits or losses, weekly operating statements shall be sent to Author with payment.

16.   Billing Credits

In all programs, houseboards, painted signs and paid advertising of the Play under the control of Producer, (except marquees, ABC and teaser ads and small ads where no credits are given other than to the title of the Play, the name(s) of the star(s) if any, the name of the theatre and/or one or more critics' quotes), credit shall be given to Author.

The name of Author shall be in type at least sixty percent (60%) of the size, boldness and prominence of the title of the Play or the size and prominence of the star(s) whichever shall be larger. No names except that of the star(s) or a director of prominence shall be more prominent than Author's name, and no names other than the star(s) or Producers shall appear above that of the Author.

Wherever credits are accorded in connection with the Play in a so-called "billing box" pursuant to which the Author is entitled to credit, the size of both the Author and Producer's credits shall be determined by the size of the title of the Play in such "billing box" and will appear only in the billing box.

No inadvertent failure to accord the billing herein provided shall be deemed a breach hereof, unless the same shall not be remedied promptly upon written notice from Author to Producers.

17. House Seats

Producers shall hold one (1) pair of adjoining house seats for Author or his designee, for all Off-Broadway or middle theatre performances of the Play in New York City, and two (2) pairs for each Broadway performances located in the first ten (10) rows in the center section of the orchestra. Additionally, Author shall have the right to purchase four (4) additional pairs of seats in good locations for Opening Night. Such house seats shall be held seventy-two hours (72) prior to the scheduled performance and shall be paid for at the regularly established box office prices. Author acknowledges and agrees that the theatre tickets made available hereunder cannot, except in accordance with the regulations promulgated by the office of the Attorney General of the State of New York, be resold at a premium or otherwise, and that complete and accurate records will be maintained by him, which may be inspected at reasonable times by a duly designated representative of Producers and/or the Attorney General of the State of New York, with respect to the disposition of all tickets made available hereunder.

18. Radio and Television Exploitation

Producers shall have the right to authorize one or more radio and/or television presentations of excerpts from Producers' production of the Play (each such presentation not to exceed fifteen (15) minutes) for the sole purpose of exploiting and publicizing the production of the Play, including presentation on the Antoinette Perry Award (Tony) television program and similar award programs, provided Producers receive no compensation or profits (other than reimbursement for out of pocket expenses), directly or indirectly, for authorizing such radio or television presentations.

19. Right of Assignment

Producers shall have the right to assign this Agreement to a partnership in which Producers, or an entity controlled by Producers, are a general partner; to a joint venture or to a corporation in which either Producer is one of the controlling principals. Any other assignments will require the Producers' approval in writing.

20. Ownership of Copyright and Ideas Contributed by Third Parties

The Author shall control the uses and disposition of the Play except as otherwise provided hereunder. All rights in and to the Play not expressly granted to Producers hereunder are hereby reserved to Author and for Author's use and disposition. All ideas with respect to the Play, whether contributed by the director, or a third party, shall belong to Author. Any copyright of the Play, including any extensions or renewals thereof throughout the world, shall be in the name of the Author.

21. Limitations on Use of Costume and Scenery Designs

Pursuant to the rules and regulations of the United Scenic Artists, Designing Artists and Theatrical Costume Designers' Contract, Author undertakes and agrees that she will not sell, lease, license or authorize the use of any of the original designs of scenery and costumes created by the designers under the standard Scenic Designing Artists and Theatrical Costume Designing Contracts for the productions, without the designer's consent to Producers' consent.

22. Notices

Any notice to be given hereunder shall be sent by registered or certified mail, return receipt requested, or telegraph or cable addressed to the parties at their respective addresses given herein, or by delivering the same personally to the parties at the addresses first set forth herein. Any party may designate a different address by notice so given. Copies of all notices shall be sent to: Tanner Gilbert Propp & Sterner, 99 Park Avenue, New York, New York 10016, Attention: Donald C. Farber, Esq.

23. Arbitration

Any dispute or controversy arising under, out of, or in connection with this Agreement or the making or validity thereof, its interpretation or any breach thereof, shall be determined and settled by arbitration by one arbitrator who shall be selected by mutual agreement of the parties hereto, in New York City, pursuant to the Rules of the American Arbitration Association. The arbitrator is directed to award to the prevailing party reasonable attorneys' fees, costs and disbursements, including reimbursement for the cost of witnesses, travel and subsistence during the arbitration hearings. Any award rendered shall be final and conclusive upon the parties and a judgment thereon may be entered by the appropriate court of the forum having jurisdiction.

24. Applicable Law, Entire Agreement

This Agreement shall be deemed to have been made in New York, New York and shall be governed by New York law applicable to agreements duly executed and to be performed wholly within the State of New York. This Agreement shall be the complete and binding agreement between the parties and may not be amended except by an agreement in writing signed by the parties hereto.

25. Successors and Assigns

The terms and conditions of this Agreement shall be binding upon the respective executors, administrators, successors and assigns of the parties hereto, provided, however, that none of the parties hereto shall, except as otherwise herein provided, have the right, without the written consent of the parties, to assign his or her rights or obligations hereunder, except the right to receive the share of the proceeds, if any, from the Play, payable to such party hereunder.

26. Computation of Paid Public Performances

All computations of "paid public performances" pursuant to any part of this Agreement shall not include any developmental performances in the computation.

IN WITNESS WHEREOF, the parties hereto have hereunto set their hands the day and year first above written.

_____

Producer

_____

Producer

_____

Author

Co-Production Agreement

This agreement is made and entered into on this 1st day of June, 1988, by and among Abe Abe, residing at 11 Pine Street, New York, New York 12345, Cal Cal, residing at 23 Oak Street New York, New York 23456 and Don Don, residing at 34 Fir Street New York, New York 34567 (hereinafter collectively referred to as the "General Partners").

All pronouns and any variations thereof shall be deemed to refer to the masculine, feminine, neuter, singular or plural, as the identity of the person, persons, firm or firms, corporation or corporations may require.

The General Partners desire to co-produce a play presently entitled "No Way" (the "Play"), written by Flo Flo (the "Author") and hereby agree as follows:

1. Formation of Joint Venture:

(a) The General Partners hereby form a joint venture for the production and presentation of the Play on the speaking stage in the United States, Canada and elsewhere and for the exploitation of the rights held or to be acquired therein by the General Partners (the "Joint Venture"). The General Partners shall cause a limited partnership to be organized pursuant to the laws of the State of New York under the name of the "No Way Limited Partnership" (the "Partnership") to produce the Play and to exploit the rights therein obtained from the Author. Unless otherwise agreed among them by a majority vote, the General Partners shall be the sole general partners of the Partnership. The parties contributing to the capital thereof will be the limited partners of the Partnership ("Limited Partners"). The limited partnership agreement ("Partnership Agreement") shall be drawn by counsel for the production, Donald C. Farber, Esq., Tanner Gilbert Propp & Sterner, 99 Park Avenue, New York, New York 10016, in the form customarily used by counsel for the theatrical production entities formed as limited partnerships in New York.

(b) The General Partners have entered or will enter into an option agreement (the "Production Contract") with the Author, whereby they have acquired or will acquire certain rights to produce and present the Play on the speaking stage.

2. Capitalization

(a) The capitalization of the Partnership (the "Original Capital") shall not exceed Five Hundred Thousand Dollars ($500,000.00), with no overcall provision to be provided in the Partnership Agreement. The Original Capital required for the Partnership will be determined after the General Partners have decided whether to present a regional theatre production of the Play prior to the New York opening.

(b) The General Partners shall be responsible for furnishing or raising the Original Capital.

(c) The General Partners contemplate producing the Play to open in an off-Broadway theatre in New York City and have also obtained or will obtain the option of producing the Play in a regional theatre either in lieu of or prior to any other production of the Play by the General Partners.

(d) To the extent that a General Partner intends to raise his portion of the Original Capital from third parties, he agrees that he will do so in a manner which: (i) will not violate any federal or state securities law; and (ii) will not require or constitute a "public offering," as that term is defined in the Securities and Exchange Act of 1933 and the rules and regulations of the Securities and Exchange Commission thereunder. It is currently anticipated that Original Capital will be solicited from residents of the State of New York and the Commonwealth of Pennsylvania.

(e) Each General Partner agrees that he will indemnify the other and the Partnership from and against any claims, liabilities, losses, costs and expenses (including reasonable counsel fees) arising from or by reason of any breach, claimed breach, by said General Partner of any of the foregoing provisions of this paragraph "2."

3. Partnership Agreement:

With respect to the distribution of net profits between the General and Limited Partners the partnership agreement shall provide, inter alia, that:

(a) The Limited Partners shall contribute the Original Capital to the Partnership; and

(b) Each Limited Partner will be entitled to receive sums equal to that proportion of fifty percent (50%) of the net profits of the Partnership, as the term "net profits" shall be defined in the Partnership Agreement, as his contribution bears to the Original Capital.

(c) The General Partners will be entitled to receive sums equal to the remaining fifty percent (50%) of the net profits of the Partnership. The net profits shall first be used to repay the Limited Partners the Original Capital before such profits are shared with the General Partners.

(d) If any star or other person is entitled to receive any part of the gross receipts or net profits of the Partnership, the same shall be deemed to be an expense of the Partnership and shall be deducted before computing the net profits to be divided among the General and Limited Partners.

4. Net Profits and Losses:

(a) The share of any net profits of the Partnership, as that term shall be defined in the Partnership agreement, due the General Partners, shall be divided among them as follows:

(i) Such sums as may equal ten percent (10%) of the net profits will be divided equally by and among the General Partners, regardless of the number of General Partners included in the Partnership at the time such profits are distributed;

(ii) Such sums as may equal the balance of the net profits due the General Partners, after any deduction of interests in net profits which may be assigned by the General Partners pursuant to paragraph 4 (iii) hereof, will be divided proportionately by and among the General Partners on the basis of the respective proportion of Original Capital furnished or raised by each General Partner;

(iii) Interests in net profits due the General Partners may be assigned to third parties upon the approval of a majority of the General Partners, and in such event assigned interests will be deducted from the share of net profit due the General Partners before distribution of same to the General Partners. A General Partner may also freely assign his respective interest in net profits due such assigning General Partner. Any net losses of the Partnership over and above the Original Capital shall be borne equally by the General Partners. If any General Partner shall pay more than his proportionate share of any such loss, the other General Partners shall indemnify him for his respective shares thereof.

5.   Control by General Partners:

The General Partners shall have complete control, in their sole discretion, of the production of the Play and the exploitation of all rights held or acquired therein. Each of them agrees to render, in connection with the Play, such services as are customarily rendered by theatrical producers and to devote such time thereto as may be necessary. It is hereby agreed, however, that the General Partners may engage in other businesses and activities, including, but not limited to, other theatrical productions. Unless otherwise specifically agreed to either in this or any other written agreement by and among the General Partners, it is understood and agreed that all artistic and management related decisions to be made by the General Partners in connection with the Play are subject to the prior majority approval of the General Partners, subject to the conditions contained in paragraph "9" hereof.

6.   Staff:

The parties hereto agree that in connection with the production of the Play the following persons or entities shall be employed or retained for the responsibilities set forth by their respective names on such terms as are agreed upon by the General Partners and such persons, such terms to be negotiated in good faith and approval of which will not be unreasonably withheld by any General Partner:

(a) General Manager—Henry Henry

(b) Legal Counsel—Donald C. Farber, Esq. Tanner Gilbert Propp Sterner 99 Park Avenue New York, New York 10016

Approval by the majority of the General Partners shall be required to engage additional or substitute personnel, subject to the conditions contained in paragraph "9" hereof.

7. Bank Accounts:

All monies contributed to the Partnership prior to formation thereof, including Original Capital, front money and loans, shall be held in a special bank account in trust until actually employed for pre-production or production purposes of this particular theatrical production or returned to the investor or investors thereof, such special bank account to be in the name of the Partnership.

Checks drawn on the capital account shall require the signature of two (2) General Partners. Checks drawn on the General Manager's account, which shall have a maximum balance at all times as agreed upon by a majority of the General Partners, shall require the signature of one (1) General Partner or the signature of the General Manager.

8. Pre-Production Expenses:

All pre-production expenses, if any, incurred or to be incurred by the General Partners in connection with the production of the Play shall be determined by written agreement among a majority of the General Partners, and shall be shared equally by the General Partners. All reimbursable pre-production expenses shall be repaid, promptly upon formation of the Partnership, to the individual General Partners who have expended same. It is presently estimated that the pre-production expenses will be approximately $50,000.00.

9. Management and Artistic Decisions:

The General Partners shall consult with one another as to all matters relating to the Partnership and shall attempt to reach agreeable decisions. No contracts, agreements or commitments of any kind or character relating to the Partnership, the production of the Play, or the exploitation of the rights held in the Play, shall be entered into except after consultation among the General Partners. Should the General partners fail to obtain a majority approval on any management-related matter pertaining to the production of the Play, as distinguished from artistic matters, the decision of an arbitrator, pursuant to paragraph "18" hereof, shall be binding upon all of them. In the event of deadlock among the General Partners on any matter concerning any artistic aspect of the production of the Play, the decision of the director engaged for the production affected by such decision shall be binding upon all of them.

10. Compensation of General Partners:

The General Partners shall receive an aggregate management fee equal to two percent (2%) of the gross weekly box office receipts of each company presenting the Play. This fee shall be shared equally among the General Partners.

11. Office Facilities:

The General Partners shall furnish office facilities for the Partnership's production of the Play, for which they will receive one hundred fifty dollars ($150) per week commencing two weeks (2) prior to the beginning of rehearsals of each company of the Play, and continuing for two weeks (2) after the close of each such company. All expenses of the Play customarily covered by a cash office allowance shall be chargeable to such cash office allowance.

12. Billing:

The General Partners agree that they shall receive the following billing credit, in letters of equal size, color, boldness and prominence, in connection with all presentations of the Play hereunder: "Abe Abe, Cal Cal and Don Don Present."

Any modification of the above, including the addition of other persons, shall require the unanimous written consent of the General Partners.

13. Books And Records:

The General Partners shall have equal access to the books and records of the Joint Venture and the Partnership, which books and records shall be kept either at the office of the General Manager or at the office of the accountants for the Joint Venture.

14. Abandonment of Production:

In the event there is at any time a disagreement among the General Partners as to whether to abandon the production of the Play or any further efforts to turn to account the rights held by the Partnership, or both, then the General Partner desiring to abandon all participation in the further profits and losses of the Partnership may do so by delivering a written statement of resignation as a General Partner to the General

Partners desiring to continue the activities or the Partnership. The party or parties wishing to continue (the "continuing party") shall assume complete control of the production and presentation of the Play commencing one week subsequent to the Sunday of the week in which the party seeking to terminate the run (the "retiring party") shall have given notice thereof (the "termination date"), and the continuing party shall thereafter bear all the expenses and liabilities of the production of the Play and be entitled to receive, and divide, if applicable, all of the General Partners' share of the net profits in connection therewith as well as the management fee and cash allowance. The continuing party shall indemnify the retiring party from all liability incurred after the takeover and shall evidence such indemnity by appropriate instruments. The retiring party shall forfeit all right, title and interest in and to the further production of the Play, and the proceeds from the production of the Play, commencing with the termination date, but this shall not affect the retiring party's entitlement to proceeds completely accrued prior to the termination date but not yet received, nor shall the retiring party's pro rata share in proceeds derived from the exploitation of motion picture and subsidiary rights be reduced or affected, if the Partnership's right to share therein shall have been acquired as a result of performances prior to the termination date. Similarly, the retiring party shall be liable for any losses accrued to the date of the termination.

15. Termination of Joint Venture:

The Joint Venture shall terminate when the Partnership has terminated and all options to produce the Play and all rights to participate in proceeds from the Play granted the Joint Venture have terminated.

16. Assignment:

No General Partner may assign this Agreement or any rights therein without the prior written consent of all of the other General Partners, except that a General Partner may freely assign his financial interest in the Joint Venture or Partnership, but such assignment shall not relive the assignor of his duties and obligations except to the extent duly performed by the assignee.

17. Arbitration:

Any and all disputes, claims and controversies arising out of or relating to any provision of this agreement, or the breach thereof, shall be settled by arbitration in New York City, before a single arbitrator, in accordance with the rules, then obtaining, of the American Arbitration Association, and award rendered in such proceeding shall be binding and conclusive upon the General Partners. The General Partners hereby consent to the jurisdiction of the Supreme Court of the State of New York for the purpose of enforcing the award of an arbitrator pursuant hereto.

18. Notices:

All notices and other communications provided for or permitted herein shall be in writing, and mailed by registered or certified mail, return receipt requested, to the party entitled or required to received the same, at such party's address hereinabove set forth or at such other address as such party shall designate by notice given pursuant to this Paragraph 18. A copy of all notice given to any party shall be sent to Tanner Gilbert Propp & Sterner, 99 Park Avenue, New York, New York 10016, attention: Donald C. Farber, Esq. and to the General Manager.

All such notices, and other communications shall be deemed given when mailed in accordance with this paragraph "18".

19. Entire Agreement; Waiver; Remedies:

This agreement contains the entire understanding among the General Partners concerning the subject matter hereof, and may not be changed, modified, or altered, nor any of its provisions waived, except by an agreement in writing signed by all the General Partners. A waiver by any General Partner of any of the terms or conditions of this agreement, or of any breach thereof, shall not be deemed a waiver of such term or condition hereof, or of any subsequent breach thereof. All rights and remedies by this agreement reserved to a General Partner shall be cumulative and shall not be in limitation of any other right or remedy which such General Partner may have at law, in equity or otherwise.

20. Binding Effect:

This agreement shall be binding upon an inure to the benefit of the General Partners and their respective heirs, executors, administrators, distributees, successors, and permitted assigns.

21. Governing Law:

This agreement shall be construed in accordance with, and subject to, the laws of the State of New York, applicable to contracts made and to be performed entirely thereon.

22. Descriptive Headings:

Descriptive headings are for convenience only, and shall in no way define, limit or affect this agreement.

IN WITNESS WHEREOF, the parties have executed this agreement on the day and year first above written.

_____

_____

_____

Appendix C

Budget for a Musical

"PAGEANT"

ESTIMATED PRE-OPENING EXPENSES
FOR 299 SEAT OFF-BROADWAY THEATRE
3 WEEK REHEARSAL AND 2 WEEK PREVIEW

PHYSICAL PRODUCTION

Scenery—(Build, Paint, Flameproof)	$25,000	
Furniture, Props, Set Dressing	5,000	
Drapes, Curtains, Masking	7,500	
Costumes & Accessories	10,000	
Wigs	1,000	
Electric—Rental	6,000	
Electric Supplies	3,000	
Sound Equipment—Rental	4,000	
Recording Costs, Etc.	1,000	
Music Instrument & Stand Rental	2,000	
Put-In Crew	6,000	
Shop Prep	1,500	
Work Calls	2,000	
Stage Preparation & Restoration	1,000	
Carting & Trucking	1,000	
		$76,000

REHEARSAL AND PREVIEW SALARIES

Cast	12,000
Understudies	1,400

Dance Captain Payment	140
Stage Managers	5,125
AEA Vacation Pay Accrual	745
Musicians - Leader	2,100
- Sidemen	2,800
A.F. of M. Vacation	390
Head Carpenter	900
Head Electrician	900
Prop Dept. Head	750
Sound Operator	900
Follow Spot Operators	600
Wardrobe - Supervisor	900
- Assistant/Dresser	750
Hair/Wig Dresser	750
General Manager	5,250
Company Manager	3,300
Press Agent	3,300
Attorney (Previews)	300
Accountant (Previews)	500
Box Office—Preliminary	1,400
House Staff—Preliminary	800
	46,000

FEES

Director/Choreographer	5,300
Set Designer	2,500
Costume Designer	2,000
Lighting Designer	2,000
Sound Designer	1,500
Wig & Hair Design & Style	1,500
Production Manager	2,000
Musical Director	2,000
Music Preparation	1,000
General Manager	4,000
Attorney	7,500
Accountant	2,500
Casting Director	1,500
Asst. to Director	1,500
Asst's to Designers	3,200
	40,000

PROMOTION, PUBLICITY AND ADVERTISING

Newspaper Advertising	30,000
Media Advertising—Radio	22,000

Logo Design, Mechanical & Prep.	3,000	
Window Cards	1,500	
One Sheets & Distribution	4,500	
Marquees, Signs, Boards, etc.	3,500	
Photographs	1,500	
Press Agent Expenses	1,500	
Printing & Mailing	1,000	
Special Promotion	1,500	
		70,000

ADMINISTRATIVE AND GENERAL

Scripts & Music Repro.	1,000	
Casting & Auditions	1,500	
League Dues	60	
Rehearsal Halls	4,000	
Theatre Rent (Set-Up & Rehearsals)	3,750	
Theatre Expenses During Set-Up/Previews	2,500	
Theatre Rent (Previews)	7,000	
Theatre Service Package (Previews)	5,600	
Producer Office Expense	3,150	
Gen. Mgr. Office Expense	1,400	
Tickets	750	
Program Expenses	500	
Union Pensions	3,500	
Union Health Insurance	5,000	
Payroll Taxes	8,500	
Business Taxes	650	
Computer Payroll & Checks	640	
Insurance	10,000	
Legal Disbursements	1,500	
Developmental Expenses	10,000	
Obligations (Buy-Outs)	5,000	
Opening Night Expenses	3,000	
Departmental Expenses	2,000	
Miscellaneous	5,000	
		86,000

TOTAL ESTIMATED DIRECT PRODUCTION COSTS $318,000

ADVANCES (NON-RETURNABLE)

Authors	1,500	
Theatre	14,000	
		15,500

TOTAL ESTIMATED PRODUCTION COSTS WITH ADVANCES	$333,500

BONDS AND DEPOSITS (Returnable)

AEA Bond	9,900	
ATPAM Bond	3,600	
Theatre Deposit	3,000	
		$16,500

SUB-TOTAL	$350,000

RESERVES

General Reserve (Not Incl. Preview Income)	75,000	
Reserve for Post Opening Advertising	25,000	
		100,000

TOTAL ESTIMATED MINIMUM PRODUCTION CAPITALIZATION	$450,000

* *

"PAGEANT"
ESTIMATED WEEKLY OPERATING EXPENSES
FOR 299 SEAT OFF-BROADWAY THEATRE
BASED ON A GROSS OF $43,000

SALARIES AND FEES

Cast	3,185
Understudies	910
Dance Captain Payment	45
Stage Manager	540
First Asst. Stage Manager	540
AEA Vacation Pay Accrual	210
Musicians - Leader	600
- Sidemen	800
A.F. of M. Vacation	85
Head Carpenter	350
Head Electrician	350
Prop Dept. Head	300
Sound Operator	350
Follow Spot Operator	240
Wardrobe - Supervisor	350
- Assistant/Dresser	240

Hair/Wig Dresser	300	
General Manager	800	
Company Manager	545	
Press Agent	545	
Attorney	150	
Accountant	250	
Casting	100	
Musical Director	100	
Designers	315	
		12,200

ADVERTISING AND PUBLICITY

Newspaper Advertising	6,000	
Media Advertising—Radio	1,500	
Photographs	25	
Press Agent Expenses	150	
Printing & Mailing	25	
Special Promotion	300	
		8,000

ADMINISTRATIVE AND GENERAL

Tickets	125	
Program Maintenance, Inserts, Etc.	20	
Producer Office Expense	450	
Gen. Mgr. Office Expense	200	
Union Pensions	705	
Union Health Insurance	890	
Payroll Taxes	1,640	
Business Taxes	340	
Computer Payroll & Checks	55	
Insurance	990	
Rentals - Electrics	975	
- Sound	435	
- Instrument & Stand	325	
Costume Cleaning & Ward. Dept. Exp.	250	
Hair & Wig Expenses	150	
Departmental Expenses	200	
Miscellaneous	150	
		7,900

THEATRE RENT AND EXPENSES

Rental Guarantee	3,500	
Service Package	2,800	
Utilities, Air Conditioning, Etc.	1,000	
		7,300

TOTAL ESTIMATED FIXED WEEKLY OPERATING
   EXPENSES $35,400

ROYALTIES AND PERCENTAGES		At Gross	$43,000
Authors	- 6.0%	(P:7.5%)	2,580
Director/Choreographer	- 3.5%	(P:4.0%)	1,505
Producer	- 2.0%	(P:3.0%)	860
Original Production Co.	- 1.0%	(P:1.0%)	430
TOTAL ROYALTIES	- 12.5%		5,375
Theatre Percentage Participation	- 5.0%		2,150
			7,525

BREAK EVEN
TOTAL ESTIMATED WEEKLY RUNNING EXPENSE
BASED ON GROSS OF $43,000 $42,925

Projection of Estimated Weekly Operating Profit and (Loss)
Based on Capacity Gross of $62,500
Fixed Expenses of $31,900

UNTIL RECOUPMENT		BREAK EVEN		
GROSS	$34,500	$43,000	$46,875	$50,000
THEATRE SHARE	3,500	5,650	5,844	6,000
COMPANY SHARE	31,000	37,350	41,031	44,000
FIXED EXPENSES	30,930	31,900	32,110	32,400
ROYALTIES 12.50%	-WAIVED-	5,375	5,859	6,250
NET	70	75	3,062	5,350
PERCENT OF CAPACITY	55	69	75	80
NET/GROSS — %	0	0	7	11
GROSS	53,125	56,250	59,375	62,500
THEATRE SHARE	6,156	6,313	6,469	6,625
COMPANY SHARE	46,969	49,938	52,906	55,875
FIXED EXPENSES	32,400	32,400	32,400	32,400
ROYALTIES 12.50%	6,641	7,031	7,422	7,813
NET	7,928	10,506	13,084	15,663
PERCENT OF CAPACITY	85	90	95	100
NET/GROSS — %	15	19	22	25

At capacity, it would take 31.6 weeks to repay $495,000.
At capacity, it would take 28.7 weeks to repay $450,000.
BREAK EVEN POINT: 68.8% OF CAPACITY

Projection of Estimated Weekly Operating Profit and (Loss)
Based on Capacity Gross of $62,500
Fixed Expenses of $32,400

AFTER RECOUPMENT	STOP CLAUSE		BREAK EVEN	
GROSS	$35,000	$43,000	$48,500	$50,000
THEATRE SHARE	5,250	5,650	5,925	6,000
COMPANY SHARE	29,750	37,350	42,575	44,000
FIXED EXPENSES	31,900	32,400	32,400	32,400
ROYALTIES 15.50%	-WAIVED-	6,665	7,518	7,750
PRE-PARTICIPATION NET	(2,150)	(1,715)	2,658	3,850
NET PARTICIPATIONS (7%)	0	(120)	186	270
EFFECTIVE NET	(2,150)	(1,595)	2,471	3,581
(UBT) 4.00%	0	(64)	99	143
PROFIT OR (LOSS)	(2,150)	(1,531)	2,373	3,437
PERCENT OF CAPACITY	56	69	78	80
MARGIN/INCOME – %	(6)	(4)	5	7

				CAPACITY
GROSS	53,125	56,250	59,375	62,500
THEATRE SHARE	6,156	6,313	6,469	6,625
COMPANY SHARE	46,969	49,938	52,906	55,875
FIXED EXPENSES	32,400	32,400	32,400	32,400
ROYALTIES 15.50%	8,234	8,719	9,203	9,688
PRE-PARTICIPATION NET	6,334	8,819	11,303	13,788
NET PARTICIPATIONS (7%)	443	617	791	965
EFFECTIVE NET	5,891	8,201	10,512	12,822
(UBT) 4.00%	236	328	420	513
PROFIT	5,655	7,873	10,091	12,309
PERCENT OF CAPACITY	85	90	95	100
Margin/Income – %	11	14	17	20

Budget for a Musical Review (Cabaret)

"PARTY OF ONE"

ESTIMATED PRE-OPENING EXPENSES
FOR 299 SEAT CABARET THEATRE
1 WEEK REHEARSALS AND 1 WEEK PREVIEWS

PHYSICAL PRODUCTION

Scenery (Build, Paint, Flameproof)	$ 500	
Furniture, Props, Set Dressing	1,000	
Drapes, Curtains, Masking	750	
Costumes & Accessories	2,500	
Electric—Rental (Supplementary)	750	
Electric Supplies	1,000	
Sound Equipment—Rental	1,000	
Music Instrument (Piano) Rental	1,000	
Put-In Crew	2,000	
Theatre Prep, Shop Prep & Work Calls	1,000	
Carting & Trucking	500	
		$12,000

REHEARSAL AND PREVIEW SALARIES

Cast	2,920
Understudies	365
Stage Manager	1,365
Asst. S.M./Understudy	820
AEA Vacation Pay Accrual	220

Musicians - Leader	1,200	
- Sidemen	800	
- Doubles, Etc.	200	
A.F. of M. Local 802 Vacation	180	
Electrician	525	
Props/Wardrobe	450	
Sound Operator	525	
Follow Spot Operators	0	
General Manager	2,250	
Company Manager	1,635	
Press Agent	2,725	
Attorney (Previews)	200	
Accountant (Previews)	300	
Box Office—Preliminary	420	
House Staff—Preliminary	400	
		17,500

FEES

Director	3,375	
Set Designer (See Light Des.)	1,000	
Costume Designer	2,000	
Lighting Designer	1,600	
Sound Designer	1,600	
Musical Director	2,000	
Music Preparation	0	
General Manager	5,000	
Attorney	8,500	
Accountant	3,000	
Casting Director	0	
Production Assistant	950	
Asst's to Designers (C=1,L=2)	975	
		30,000

PROMOTION, PUBLICITY AND ADVERTISING

Newspaper Advertising	14,000	
Media Advertising—Radio	17,000	
Logo Design & Mechanical/Prep.	1,500	
Window Cards	1,000	
Flyers & Distribution	500	
Signs, Boards, Banner, etc.	1,500	
Photographs	1,500	
Press Agent Expenses	2,000	
Special Promotion	1,000	
		40,000

ADMINISTRATIVE AND GENERAL

Scripts & Music Repro.	200
Casting & Auditions	500
League Fee	60
Rehearsal Halls	0
Theatre Rent (Set-Up & Rehearsals)	1,500
Theatre Expenses During Set-Up/Previews	800
Theatre Rent (Previews)	3,000
Theatre Service Package (Previews)	2,400
Producer Office Expense	2,000
Gen. Mgr. Office Expense	800
Telephone & Telegraph	500
Travel Expenses	4,000
Author Trans. & Per Diem	5,500
Tickets	300
Program Expenses	350
Union Pensions	1,480
Union Health Insurance	1,830
Payroll Taxes	3,275
Business Taxes	270
Computer Payroll & Checks	555
Insurance	4,850
Legal Disbursements	1,000
Developmental Expenses	12,000
Opening Night Expenses	1,000
Departmental Expenses	500
Miscellaneous	2,330

	51,000

TOTAL ESTIMATED DIRECT PRODUCTION COSTS	$150,500

ADVANCES (NON-RETURNABLE)

Authors	500
Director	1,125
Theatre	12,000

	13,625

TOTAL ESTIMATED PRODUCTION COSTS WITH ADVANCES	$164,125

BONDS AND DEPOSITS (RETURNABLE)

AEA Bond	6,385
ATPAM Bond	3,115
Theatre Deposit	5,000

	14,500

SUB-TOTAL	$178,625

RESERVES

General Reserve (Not Incl. Preview Income)	26,375	
Reserve for Post Opening Advertising	20,000	
		46,375

TOTAL ESTIMATED PRODUCTION CAPITALIZATION $225,000
* *

EACH OF 50 UNITS OF INVESTMENT SUBSCRIPTION: $4,500
* *

THIS ESTIMATED PRODUCTION EXPENSE BUDGET DOES NOT
CONSTITUTE AN OFFERING. THE OFFERING CAN ONLY BE
MADE BY THE LIMITED PARTNERSHIP AGREEMENT AS AP-
PROVED BY THE ATTORNEY GENERAL.
* *

"PARTY OF ONE"

ESTIMATED WEEKLY OPERATING EXPENSES
FOR 299 SEAT CABARET THEATRE
BASED ON A GROSS OF $36,000
[IF AEA OFF-B'WAY CONTRACT]

SALARIES AND FEES

Cast	1,780
Understudies	445
Stage Manager	535
Asst. S.M./Understudy	490
AEA Vacation & Sick Pay Accrual	230
Musicians - Leader	600
- Sidemen	0
- Doubles, Etc.	100
A.F. of M. Vacation	55
Electrician	350
Props/Wardrobe	300
Sound Operator	350
Follow Spot Operators	0
General Manager	750
Company Manager	545
Press Agent	545

House Staff	525	
Attorney	200	
Accountant	300	
Musical Director	100	
Designers	300	
		8,500

ADVERTISING AND PUBLICITY

Newspaper Advertising	5,000	
Media Advertising—Radio	1,500	
Photographs	25	
Press Agent Expenses	150	
Printing & Mailing	25	
Special Promotion	300	
		7,000

ADMINISTRATIVE AND GENERAL

Tickets	300	
Program Maintenance, Inserts, Etc.	20	
Producer Office Expense	500	
Gen. Mgr. Office Expense	200	
Union Pensions	485	
Union Health Insurance	540	
Payroll Taxes	1,100	
Business Taxes	485	
Computer Payroll & Checks	55	
Insurance	800	
Rentals - Electrics	150	
- Sound	220	
- Instrument & Stand	220	
Costume Cleaning & Ward. Dept. Exp.	125	
Departmental Expenses	150	
Miscellaneous	150	
		5,500

THEATRE RENT AND EXPENSES

Rental Guarantee	3,000	
Service Package	2,400	
Theatre Expenses	200	
		5,600

TOTAL ESTIMATED FIXED WEEKLY OPERATING
EXPENSES $26,600

ROYALTIES AND PERCENTAGES		$36,000	
Author	- 6.0%	2,160	
Director	- 2.0%	720	
Producer	- 2.0%	720	
Associate Producer(s)	- 1.0%	360	
TOTAL ROYALTIES	- 11.0%	3,960	
Theatre Percentage Participation	- 15.0%	5,400	
			9,360

BREAK EVEN
TOTAL ESTIMATED WEEKLY RUNNING EXPENSE
BASED ON GROSS OF $36,000 $35,960
* *

RECAP

ESTIMATED INCOME AT CAPACITY: $52,700

ESTIMATED EXPENSES AT CAPACITY: $40,800

ESTIMATED MAXIMUM NET WEEKLY PROFIT: $11,900

BREAK EVEN POINT: 68.3% OF CAPACITY
* *

At capacity, it would take 19 weeks to recoup the investment.

NOTATIONS: THIS BREAK EVEN OF $36,000 IS BASED ON THE USE
OF THE A.E.A. OFF-BROADWAY CONTRACT SAL-
ARY RATES AND PENSION AND HEALTH BENEFIT
RATES FOR EQUITY MEMBERS.
* *

THIS ESTIMATED WEEKLY OPERATING BUDGET DOES NOT
CONSTITUTE AN OFFERING. THE OFFERING CAN ONLY BE
MADE BY THE LIMITED PARTNERSHIP AGREEMENT AS AP-
PROVED BY THE ATTORNEY GENERAL.

* *

OFFERING CIRCULAR FOR SEC REGULATION AND EXEMPTION

OFFERING CIRCULAR

$250,000 maximum ($200,000 minimum) in Limited Partnership
Interests
in

THE SHARP LIMITED PARTNERSHIP

A Limited Partnership to be formed to finance, produce
and present Off-Broadway (in a theatre with approximately
285 seats) the new musical play presently entitled:

SHARP (The "Play")

**THE UNITED STATES SECURITIES AND EXCHANGE COM-
MISSION DOES NOT PASS UPON THE MERITS OF OR GIVE
ITS APPROVAL TO ANY SECURITIES OFFERED OR THE
TERMS OF THE OFFERING, NOR DOES IT PASS UPON THE
ACCURACY OR COMPLETENESS OF ANY OFFERING CIR-
CULAR OR OTHER SELLING LITERATURE. THESE SECURI-
TIES ARE OFFERED PURSUANT TO AN EXEMPTION FROM
REGISTRATION WITH THE COMMISSION; HOWEVER, THE
COMMISSION HAS NOT MADE AN INDEPENDENT DETER-
MINATION THAT THE SECURITIES OFFERED HEREUNDER
ARE EXEMPT FROM REGISTRATION.**

	Price to Public	Underwriting Discounts or Commissions[1]	Proceeds to the Limited Partnership[2]
Per Unit Maximum	$5,000	—	$5,000
Per Unit Minimum	$4,000	—	$4,000
Total Maximum	$250,000	—	$250,000
Total Minimum	$200,000	—	$200,000

Pre-Formation Limited Partnership Interests ("Limited Partnership Interests") are being offered by Ida Ida residing at 321 West 54th Street, New York, N.Y. 10011 ("the General Partner"). The ultimate issuer will be THE SHARP LIMITED PARTNERSHIP, when formed (the "Partnership"), whose address is 321 West 54th Street, New York, New York 10011 and whose telephone number is (212) 987 0123. All monies will be held by the General Partner in a Special Account at Citibank, 46th Street & 3rd Avenue, New York, NY 10163 until the total capital contributions are raised.

THE DATE OF THIS OFFERING CIRCULAR IS _____

Date of Commencement of proposed sale to public: As soon as practicable following the filing of the Notification Form 1-A relating to this offering and terminating May 30, 1990.

THESE SECURITIES INVOLVE A HIGH DEGREE OF RISK AND PROSPECTIVE PURCHASERS SHOULD BE PREPARED TO SUSTAIN A LOSS OF THEIR ENTIRE INVESTMENT (SEE "RISK FACTORS").

THIS OFFERING CIRCULAR MAY NOT BE USED FOR A PERIOD OF MORE THAN NINE (9) MONTHS. THEREAFTER, THE ATTORNEY GENERAL OF THE STATE OF NEW YORK DOES NOT PASS ON THE MERITS OF THIS OFFERING.

NO DEALER, SALESMAN OR ANY OTHER PERSON HAS BEEN AUTHORIZED TO GIVE ANY INFORMATION OR TO MAKE ANY REPRESENTATION OTHER THAN THOSE CONTAINED IN THIS OFFERING CIRCULAR, AND IF GIVEN OR MADE, SUCH INFORMATION OR REPRESENTATIONS MUST NOT BE RELIED UPON AS HAVING BEEN AUTHORIZED BY THE GENERAL PARTNER. THIS OFFERING CIRCULAR DOES NOT CONSTITUTE AN OFFER TO SELL OR A SOLICITATION OF AN OFFER TO BUY ANY OF THE SECURITIES OFFERED HEREBY, TO ANY PERSON IN ANY JURISDICTION WHERE SUCH OFFER OR SOLICITATION WOULD BE UNLAWFUL.

FOOTNOTES:
(1) This offering has no underwriters.
(2) Before deducting expenses payable by the Issuer related to this offering, which are estimated at $15,000.
(3) Aggregate Pre-Formation Limited Partnership Interests are not actually divided into a specific number of units and monetary amounts. For purposes of convenience, they may be considered to consist of 50 "Units" of $5,000 per Unit.

THE SHARP LIMITED PARTNERSHIP
TABLE OF CONTENTS

	Page
Facing Sheet	Cover
Statement Regarding Dealers	00
Footnotes	00
Table of Contents	00
Summary of the Offering Circular	00
The Partnership	00
Risk Factors	00
The Offering	00
Additional Capital Contributions of Limited Partners (Overcall)	00
Use of Proceeds	00
Estimated Weekly Budget	00
The Play	00
The Author	00
The Director	00
The Scenic, Lighting and Costume Designers	00
The Cast	00
The General Partner	00
The Theatre	00
Production and Subsidiary Rights	00
Compensation of the General Partner (Producer)	00
Net Profits and Certain Expenses Defined	00
Return of Capital Contributions—Share of Net Profits	00
Other Financing	00
Financial Statements	00
Effect of Federal Income Taxes	00
Legal Opinions	00
Indemnification	00
Federal Securities Law	00
Part III—Exhibits	00
Signature	00

SUMMARY OF THE OFFERING CIRCULAR

The Partnership will be formed for the purpose of producing and presenting the Play and exploiting and turning to account the rights at any time held by the Partnership in connection therewith (see "THE PARTNERSHIP"). It is currently anticipated that the Play will open Off-Broadway in New York City on or before May 30, 1990.

The Partnership will be formed upon or prior to the sale of 50 Units and the receipt by the General Partner of capital contributions totaling $250,000 (or such lesser amount as the General Partner determines is sufficient to produce the play but in no event less than $200,000) (see "RISK FACTOR #5") by the filing of a duly executed Certificate of Limited Partnership in the Office of the Clerk of New York County. The Certificate shall be filed as soon as possible after the execution of the Limited Partnership Agreement by the General Partner and at least one limited partner ("Limited Partner"). The Limited Partners will receive 50% of the net profits of the Partnership and the General Partner will receive 50% of such profits.

The Partnership shall terminate upon the occurrence of any of the following: (i) the Bankruptcy, death, insanity or resignation of an individual General Partner or the dissolution, cessation of business or Bankruptcy of a corporate General Partner; (ii) the expiration of all of the Partnership's right, title and interest in the Play; (iii) a date fixed by the General Partner after abandonment of all further Partnership activities; or (iv) any other event causing the dissolution of the Partnership under the laws of the State of New York. Notwithstanding the foregoing, the Partnership shall not be dissolved upon the occurrence of the Bankruptcy, death, dissolution or withdrawal or adjudication of incompetence of a General Partner if all of the remaining General Partners elect within 30 days after such an event to continue the business of the Partnership.

The Partnership's plan of operation is: (a) to engage in pre-production activities with respect to the Play; (b) upon completion of pre-production activities, to engage in rehearsals of the Play; (c) during the rehearsal period, to begin the promotion and publicity for the Play; and (d) to produce and present the Play. For further information with respect to these matters, see "USE OF PROCEEDS."

Since the Partnership has not yet been formed, there are no income, expense or other financial statements of the Partnership presently available. For information with respect to the risks to subscribers in connection with this offering, see generally "RISK FACTORS."

THE PARTNERSHIP

The General Partner shall organize the Partnership as a New York limited partnership to raise capital contributions totalling $250,000 (or such lesser amount as the General Partner determines is sufficient to produce the play but in no event less than $200,000) and for the purpose of producing and presenting the Play and exploiting and turning to account the rights held by the Partnership therein. The capitalization requirement is, in the opinion of the General Partner, sufficient to mount a production of the Play in an Off-Broadway theatre containing approximately 284 seats.

If 50 Units have not been sold by May 30, 1990 (the date to which the rights to produce the play have been extended in accordance with the agreement of May 30, 1988), the offering will cease and all capital contributions theretofore received will be returned with accrued interest, if any, except capital contributions which have been expended by consent of individual subscribers who have waived their right of refund (see "RISK FACTOR #5").

The General Partner will have sole and complete authority over the management and operations of the Partnership. The General Partner in his sole discretion may purchase Units of Limited Partnership Interests in the Partnership and participate therein as a Limited Partner. However, at present the General Partner has not determined whether he will so participate as a Limited Partner or the extent of any such participation. The General Partner will assign to the Partnership, upon formation, certain rights in the Play which he has acquired on behalf of the Partnership. Upon formation, the Partnership will assume all obligations and liabilities incurred by the General Partner in acquiring such stage production and all other rights assigned to the Partnership. For additional information on the rights acquired by the General Partner and the division of proceeds therefrom, see "PRODUCTION AND SUBSIDIARY RIGHTS."

The executive offices of the Partnership will be: c/o Ira Ira, 321 West 54th Street, New York, New York 10011, telephone number: (212) 987-0123, unless otherwise designated by the General Partner.

RISK FACTORS

(1) Based on the "Review of the 1987–1988 Theatrical Season" released by the New York State Department of Law, of the Off-Broadway productions subject to New York State's Theatrical Syndication Financing Act during the 1987–1988 Season, a substantial number of productions reported losses and unrecovered costs.

(2) Based on Partnership capitalization of $250,000 and the estimated weekly expenses for the production of the Play, (see "USE OF PROCEEDS" and "ESTIMATED WEEKLY BUDGET"), and assuming the Play is presented at prevailing box office scale in a 285-seat Off-Broadway theatre with potential gross weekly box office receipts of $45,000 the Play must run for approximately 14½ weeks (116 performances) to a full capacity house in order to return to the Limited Partners their initial capital contributions, or for a longer period of time if presented at less than full house capacity. Based on a Partnership Capitalization of $200,000 the play under such circumstances must run for a period of twelve (12) weeks (96 performances) to a full capacity house in order to return the Limited Partners their initial Capital Contributions. The substantial majority of the plays produced for the Off-Broadway stage during the 1987–1988 season failed to run for 14½ weeks. Of those that did, few played to capacity audiences throughout their run.

(3) There is no assurance that the Play will be an economic success even if the Play receives critical acclaim.

(4) These securities should not be purchased unless the subscriber is prepared for the possibility of total loss and is able to afford such total loss. The sole business of the Partnership will be the production of the Play. In such a venture the risk of loss is especially high in contrast with the prospect for the realization of any profits.

(5) An individual subscriber may agree to the use of his capital contribution prior to full capitalization of the Partnership, and either retain or waive his absolute right of refund in the event of abandonment prior to the production of the Play. A subscriber who agrees to earlier use may sustain unlimited liability for production debts incurred prior to formation of the Partnership. Subscribers waiving refund may lose all or part of their respective investments, without a production of the Play having been presented, if insufficient funds are raised to complete the offering, or if the offering is not completed for any other reason. Subscribers *not* waiving refund must rely solely on the ability of the

General Partner to reimburse them for their expended capital contributions, which might exceed the assets of the General Partner and result in a total loss to such subscribers. There is a distinct disadvantage to waiving such refund because persons who do so risk the loss of their entire investment even if the Partnership is never formed or the Play is abandoned prior to production.

(6) In the event the capital contributions raised through this offering are insufficient to produce the Play as contemplated, the General Partner may advance or cause to be advanced, or may borrow on behalf of the Partnership, additional capital. Such advances or loans are to be repaid prior to the repayment of the capital contribution of any Limited Partner. Such advances or loans might result in a considerable delay in the repayment of capital contributions, or in a complete loss to subscribers if such loans or advances equal or exceed the revenues from the production of the Play.

(7) If the Partnership receives an exemption from the requirements of filing certified accounting statements, pursuant to the New York Arts and Cultural Affairs Law, Limited Partners may be furnished with unaudited financial statements. The General Partner has not, as of the date of this Offering Circular, applied for such exemption or determined whether such application will be made.

(8) Contributions other than cash may be accepted in the form of guarantees or bonds as may be required by Actors' Equity Association, theatres and other unions or organizations, as such contributors will receive the Limited Partnership Interest allocable to the amount of bonds or guarantees contributed, and furthermore, shall have the right to be reimbursed in full prior to the return of capital to other Limited Partners.

(9) The General Partner has not previously produced a theatrical stage production, and is under no obligation to devote her full time and efforts to the Partnership's activities (see "THE GENERAL PARTNER"). This fact may affect her ability to successfully manage the production of the Play.

(10) The General Partner will receive a share of box office receipts for each week during the run of the Play, as well as other remuneration [see "COMPENSATION OF THE GENERAL PARTNER (Producer)"], and she may continue to present the Play regardless of whether the Partnership realizes any profit.

(11) No market presently exists for resale of the Limited Partnership Interests and it is unlikely that one will develop. Limited Partners

may not assign their interests without the consent of the General Partner.

(12) If 50 Units have not been sold on or before the expiration of the initial option period, or by such date as the General Partner has extended the option period (see "PRODUCTION AND SUBSIDIARY RIGHTS"), the capital contributions of the Limited Partners shall be returned promptly, with accrued interest, if any, except there shall be no return of capital contributions expended with the consent of the individual subscribers who have waived their right of refund.

(13) Partnership net profits previously distributed to the General and Limited Partners, and capital contributions previously returned to the Limited Partners (including accrued interest returned, if any), may be recalled by the General Partner for the purposes of paying any debts, taxes, liabilities or obligations of the Partnership.

(14) The General Partner, in her sole discretion, may create one or more reserves from Partnership income for the financing of one or more additional companies of the Play. As a result, the distribution of Partnership income to the Limited Partners, as a return of their capital contributions or as net profits, or both, could be delayed, and if such additional company is not financially successful, ultimately reduced.

(15) The General Partner has not contracted for certain key elements of the production, including the director, choreographer, general manager, scenic, lighting and costume designers, and the theatre.

(16) In any year in which the Partnership shall report net profits, a Limited Partner will be taxable for his proportionate share of such net profits, whether or not such net profits have been distributed to such Limited Partner.

(17) The General Partner shall have the right to cause additional persons, firms or corporations to become General Partners at any time prior to the formation of the partnership. In this event, an offer of rescission will be made to those investors who invested before the additional general partners are added.

(18) The General Partner shall have the absolute right to abandon the production of the play.

(19) The General Partner shall have the absolute right to resign as General Partner without incurring any penalties or liabilities.

(20) In addition, the General Partner alone or associated in any way with any person, firm or corporation may produce or co-produce other productions of the Play in other places and media, and may receive compensation, therefore, without any obligation whatever to account

to the Partnership or the Limited Partners; provided, however, that the Partnership shall be entitled to receive from any such producing entity the customary fees and royalties payable to it, if any, as producer of the original Play in connection with such other productions.

(21) No escrow trust or agreement has been entered into. It is customary for theatrical limited partnerships to hold limited partners' capital contributions in a special account. The General Partner shall open a special account and she shall not withdraw funds from the special account until after the total production budget has been raised and the offering is closed out. Each Limited Partner must agree to leave his or her investment in the special account opened for that purpose or the Partnership will not accept the investment.

THE OFFERING

Each of the 50 Units of Limited Partnership Interests is being offered to the public at a purchase price of five thousand dollars ($5,000), for a Partnership capitalization of $250,000. Fractional Units may, however, be issued by the General Partner. Subscribers of Units and fractional Units shall each be entitled to receive that proportion of 50% of the Partnership's net profits which their respective capital contributions bear to the total capitalization of the Partnership. Purchasers of fractional Units will be entitled to the same rights and be subject to the same obligations as purchasers of Units. The General Partner may purchase Units and will be treated as a Limited Partner to the extent of her respective purchase of such Units. In her sole discretion, the General Partner may permit certain capital contributions to be made by the posting of required performance bonds on behalf of the Partnership. The persons posting such bonds shall participate as Limited Partners and shall be entitled to a share of net profits of the Partnership based on the cost of such bonds had they been posted directly by the Partnership.

Offers to subscribe to Limited Partnership Interests are subject to acceptance by the General Partner. A capital contribution shall be payable at the time of execution and delivery to the General Partner of the Limited Partnership agreement by the subscriber. All monies raised pursuant to this offering shall be held in trust by the General Partner in a special bank account at Citibank, 46th Street & 3rd Avenue, New York, NY 10163 until actually employed for pre-production or production expenses. Prior to the sale of 50 Units, the capital contribution of a Limited Partner may only be employed for pre-production or production expenses if specifically authorized by such subscriber. If 50 Units have not been sold prior to the expiration of the option period, May 30, 1990 (see "PRODUCTION AND SUBSIDIARY RIGHTS"), all capital contributions will be promptly returned to the Limited Partners, with accrued interest, if any, except to the extent used pursuant to specific instructions permitting the use of a subscriber's funds and waiving right of refund. Limited Partnership Interests will be offered to the public by the General Partner on behalf of the Partnership, through the use of the mails, by telephone and by personal solicitation.

A copy of this Offering Circular and of the Limited Partnership Agreement for The Sharp Limited Partnership shall be presented to each potential subscriber. A potential subscriber desiring to become a Limited Partner in the Partnership must sign the Limited Partnership Agreement and indicate the amount and category of the capital contribution being made, as well as the subscriber's actual residence address (or principal place of business of a corporation, partnership, association or other entity) and social security or employer identification number. Each executed Partnership Agreement should be forwarded to the General Partner at the Partnership address and must be accompanied by a check or money order made payable to The Sharp Limited Partnership in the full amount of the capital contribution indicated on the subscription form.

With respect to the capital contributions of Limited Partners, any one of the following may also apply:

(1) An individual subscriber may agree in writing to the use of his capital contribution prior to the sale of 50 Units without waiving the absolute right of full refund on abandonment prior to the production of the Play due to an insufficiency of funds. The General Partner will be liable to such subscribers; however, such capital contributions will not be accepted in excess of the net worth of the General Partner.

(2) The individual subscriber may agree in writing to the use of his capital contribution prior to the sale of 50 Units and waive the right of refund of such contribution on abandonment prior to the production of the Play.

(3) The General Partner may accept as an investment in lieu of cash, a cash deposit for Actors' Equity, or other union bonds, or the theatre deposit.

(4) An individual subscriber may also invest in the Partnership by purchasing an assignment from a Limited Partner, provided the General Partner consents in writing to such assignment. No assignee of a Limited Partner may become a substitute Limited Partner without the written consent of the General Partner.

The General Partner reserves the right to give to any subscriber an additional participation in net profits for any reason whatever, provided such participation is payable solely from the General Partner's share of such profits, and does not affect the proportion of net profits payable to the Limited Partners.

The Partnership books and records will be maintained at the office of the Partnership c/o Ida Ida, 321 West 54th Street, New York, New York 10011.

ADDITIONAL CAPITAL CONTRIBUTIONS BY LIMITED PARTNERS (OVERCALL)

There is *no involuntary overcall* provided for in the Limited Partnership Agreement, and if additional money is needed above the capital contributions raised, the General Partner may make funds available and must do so in a manner that will not reduce the interest of the Limited Partners in the net profits of the Limited Partnership. Any additional funds advanced or loaned to the Partnership are to be repaid prior to the return of contributions of Limited Partners.

USE OF PROCEEDS

The present estimates of pre-production and production expenses, and the allocation of capital contributions made to the Partnership are as follows:

FEES:

Director	$2,500
Lighting Designer	1,124
Scenic Designer	1,247
Costumer Designer	500
Design Assistants	1,500
	$6,871

PHYSICAL PRODUCTION:

Set Construction	10,000	
Props	2,500	
Costumes	2,500	
Shoes/Boots/Wigs	1,000	
Lighting	5,000	
		$21,000

TRANSPORTATION:

Local Trucking	1,000	
Misc. Transportation	1,000	
		$2,000

REHEARSAL SALARY—3 WEEKS:

Equity	7,921	
Stage Manager	1,626	
Asst. Stg. Manager	1,104	
Company Manager	2,002	
Press Agent	1,502	
		$14,155

REHEARSAL EXPENSES:

Audition & Casting	1,000	
Scripts	500	
Rehearsal Space	2,400	
NY Hang (includes crew)	10,000	
		$13,900

PRESS/PROMOTION:

Media	60,000	
Press Agent Expense	500	
Photo Call	750	
Photo Repro.	250	
Window Cards/Heralds	3,500	
One Sheets	500	
Art work	400	
		$65,900

MISCELLANEOUS:

Legal Fee	10,000	
Insurance Deposit	1,000	
Taxes/P&W	4,000	
Departmental	2,500	

Opening Party	1,000
Misc.	2,500
Gen Mgr—Pre-Production	5,000
Gen Mgr—Rehearsal	3,750
Theatre Deposit	7,500
Office Fee	1,750
Front of house	5,000
Closing costs	5,000
Preliminary Theatre Expense	8,000
Accountant	4,000
	$61,000

TOTAL ESTIMATED PRE-PRODUCTION COSTS	$154,826
BONDS: Equity	10,468
ATPAM	5,400
RESERVE	49,306
TOTAL CAPITALIZATION	$250,000

If the total capitalization is $200,000 instead of $250,000, the Media expense will be reduced from $60,000 to $30,000 and Reserve will be reduced from $51,806 to $31,806.

As of the date of this Offering Circular, the General Partner has advanced approximately $10,500 on behalf of the Partnership (which amounts are included in the foregoing allocation of proceeds) as follows:

FEES AND ADVANCES:
General Manager $1,000
Legal Counsel 6,000

OTHER COSTS:
Administrative & Office Expenses
(including script and cassette
duplication, long distance
telephone, and office
expenses) $3,000

RIGHTS:
Authors (Advances against Royalties) 500
$10,500

All sums which have heretofore been, or shall hereafter be, advanced by the General Partner for the benefit and on behalf of the Partnership will be repaid to the General Partner from the proceeds of this offering upon the sale of 50 Units.

ESTIMATED WEEKLY BUDGET

The maximum estimated weekly operating budget pre-recoupment for the Off-Broadway run of the Play is approximately $27,700 in a theatre with a seating capacity of approximately 285 seats. During weeks in which capacity audiences are not realized, the maximum estimated weekly operating budget will be reduced. (*See* "THE AUTHOR" below for a discussion of the royalty arrangements with Author.) Based on a capitalization of $250,000, a theatre capacity of approximately 285 seats, and a gross weekly potential for box-office receipts in the amount of $45,000 the Play must have a run of approximately fourteen and a half (14½) weeks (116 performances) at full capacity (weekly estimated profit of $17,300) merely to return to the Limited Partners their initial capital contributions. Based on a capitalization of $200,000 the play must have a run of approximately twelve (12) weeks (96 performances) at full capacity to return to the Limited Partners their initial capital contributions.

The Author's (Bookwriter, Composer-Lyricist) royalty for each production of the play under Producer's management license or control, shall be 5% of the gross weekly box office receipts until recoupment of the total production costs and 6½% thereafter (subject to the provisions of the following paragraph wherein it is provided that under certain circumstances the royalty will increase to 7% of the gross after recoupment.)

If the Author and all other royalty participants, including the Producer with respect to the Producer's fee, agree to a similar waiver of one-half of their usual royalty, the Author agrees to waive one-half of his royalty, that is two and one-half percent of the gross weekly box office receipts, until recoupment of the total production costs of production (less bonds, deposits and other recoverable items) on the express condition that: 1.) Each week's operating profits are paid directly to the investors as payment toward recoupment of such total production costs; and 2.) After recoupment of such total production costs the Author's royalty shall be in an amount equal to seven percent (7%) of the gross weekly box office receipts. Producer agreed to such waiver of one-half of Producer's fee.

The Producer's fee will be in an amount equal to 2% of the gross weekly box office receipts, which will be reduced to 1% until recoupment of the total production costs in compliance with the Royalty Pool Formula above set forth. The cash office charge payable two weeks before rehearsal until two weeks after the close of the show will be in the amount of $350.00 per week.

A percentage of gross weekly box office receipts of the Off-Broadway production of the Play will be paid to the following as indicated (an asterisk indicates an estimation), subject to the royalty pool formula referred to above:

Recipient	Share of Gross Box Office Receipts	
	Pre-Recoupment	After Recoupment
Author	5%	6½%
*Director	3%	4%
*Lighting, Scenic & Costume Designers	1%	1%
General Partner	2%	2%

If Royalty Pool Formula becomes effective.

Recipient	Share of Gross Box Office Receipts	
	Pre-Recoupment	After Recoupment
Author	2½%	7%
*Director	1½%	4%
*Lighting, Scenic & Costume Designers	2½%	1%
General Partner	1%	2%

The maximum estimated weekly fixed operating costs referred to above are based on the following allocations (pre-recoupment and post-recoupment):

Salaries	$ 6,688
Taxes	1,739
Rentals of Equipment	1,800

Advertising	5,000
Theatre Rental, Office Expense, Insurance, Attorneys Fee, and Misc.	10,160
Total	$25,387

THE PLAY

"Sharp" is a new musical comedy by Bob Bob. It has two acts, one set and seven actors.

THE AUTHOR

Bob Bob, the Author (Bookwriter, Composer-Lyricist) studied play writing at New York Academy.

As Author he will be paid a royalty of 5% of the gross weekly box office receipts until recoupment of the total production costs and 6½% thereafter. If the Royalty Pool Formula becomes effective he will be paid as Author 2½% of the gross weekly box office receipts until recoupment of the total production costs and 7% thereafter.

THE DIRECTOR

As of the date of the Offering Circular the Director has not been engaged for the Off-Broadway or Middle Theatre Production.

THE SCENIC, LIGHTING, SOUND AND COSTUME DESIGNERS

As of the date of this Offering Circular, the scenic, lighting, sound and costume designers have not been engaged for the Play. However, it is anticipated that the scenic, lighting, sound and costume designers may be entitled to receive an aggregate of one percent (1%) of the gross weekly box office receipts of each company presenting the Play under the authority or control of the General Partner. In addition, an estimated aggregate fee of approximately $4,300 will be paid to these designers.

THE CAST

As of the date of this Offering Circular, none of the cast has been selected for the Play. The General Partner has approached certain possible cast members, but has no indication regarding the cost, availability or interest of any performer.

THE GENERAL PARTNER

(See "THE AUTHOR" above.) As General Partner, Ida Ida will be paid a production fee of 2% of the gross weekly box office receipts; however, if the Royalty Pool Formula becomes effective, the Producer's fees will be reduced to 1% until the recoupment of the total production costs.

THE THEATRE

As of the date of this Offering Circular, a license agreement has not been entered into for a theatre in which to present the Play. A theatre is being sought which contains approximately 285 seats and which has a potential for gross weekly box office receipts of approximately $45,000 at full capacity. It is anticipated that the theatre will be entitled to receive a license fee and staff costs of approximately $6,000 per week.

PRODUCTION AND SUBSIDIARY RIGHTS

The General Partner has acquired the option to produce the Play as an Off-Broadway (including "Middle Theatres") production, together with certain other rights to produce the Play on Broadway, on tour and the British Isles pursuant to the Production Contract dated May 30, 1988. The term of the option period will expire on May 30, 1990.

If the Producer has produced the Play as provided therein the Author agrees that the Producer shall receive an amount equal to the percentage of net receipts (regardless of when paid) specified hereinbelow received by Authors if the Play has been produced for the number of consecutive performances set forth and if before the expiration of ten

(10) years subsequent to the date of the last public performance of the Play in New York City, and of the following rights are disposed of anywhere throughout the world: motion pictures, or with respect to the Continental United States and Canada, any of the following rights; radio, television, touring performances, stock performances, Broadway performances, Off-Broadway performances, amateur performances foreign language performances, condensed tabloid versions, commercial and merchandising uses, and audio and video cassettes and discs: Ten percent (10%) if the Play shall run for at least twenty-one (21) consecutive paid performances; twenty percent (20%) if the Play shall run for at least forty-two consecutive paid performances; thirty percent (30%) if the Play shall run for at least fifty-six (56) consecutive paid performances; forty percent (40%) if the Play shall run for sixty-five (65) consecutive paid performances or more. For the purposes of computing the number of performances, provided the Play officially opens in New York City, the first paid performance shall be deemed to be the first performance, however only seven paid previews will be counted in this computation.

The above computation of the General Partner's share in subsidiary rights is set forth in the aforementioned Production Contract, a copy of which is on file and available for inspection during normal business hours at the offices of legal counsel for the Partnership: Donald C. Farber, Esq. of Tanner Propp Fersko & Sterner, 99 Park Avenue, New York, New York 10016.

The General Partner will assign to the Limited Partnership, when formed, all of the rights granted to his by the Author, including all interests in subsidiary rights and production rights pursuant to the Production contract.

COMPENSATION OF THE GENERAL PARTNER (PRODUCER)

In addition to her share of any net profits of the Partnership in the aggregate of fifty percent (50%), for which the General Partner will make no Capital Contribution, the General Partner will receive the following compensation and advantages whether or not the Partnership earns net profits:

(1) As a Producer's management fee—two percent (2%) of the gross weekly box office receipts (reduced to 1% until recoupment of the total

production costs if the Royalty Pool Formula becomes effective) for each company presenting the Play under the authority or control of the Partnership.

(2) For furnishing office space and secretarial services for the benefit of all productions of the Play, the General Partner will receive three hundred fifty ($350) dollars per week for each company presenting the Play under her authority or control. This cash office charge shall commence two (2) weeks before the commencement of rehearsals and end two (2) weeks after the close of each company presenting the Play under the authority or control of the Partnership. The offices of the Partnership will be: c/o Ida Ida, 321 West 54th Street, New York, New York 10011, and such offices will not be used exclusively for the activities of the Partnership. To the extent that charges received from the Partnership by the General Partner for office space and other items furnished by her exceed their own cost, the General Partner will receive additional compensation.

In the event that the General Partner finds it necessary to perform any services usually performed by a third person, (see reference to acting a role to above in "CAST") the General Partner may, if she so desires, receive the compensation for such services which the third party would have received had such third party directly performed the required services. In any event, such compensation must be an amount reasonable for the rendering of such services. As of the date of this Offering Circular, the General Partner has not made any plans, arrangements, commitments or undertakings to perform services for the Partnership which would otherwise be provided by a third person. In the event that the General Partner deems it advisable, she may license theatre space from a partnership, corporation or other entity in which the General Partner may have an interest, providing that the terms of such license are reasonable and no less favorable than the terms would be if it were rented from a third person in an arms-length transaction.

The General Partner will receive no compensation, other than that stated above, for any services, equipment or facilities customarily rendered or furnished by a theatrical stage producer; nor will the General Partner receive concessions of cash, property or anything of value from persons rendering services or supplying goods to the Partnership.

NET PROFITS AND CERTAIN EXPENSES DEFINED

The following terms are defined in the Limited Partnership Agreement in the following manner:

The term "net profits" shall mean the excess of gross receipts over all "production," "running" and "other expenses," as those terms are defined in the Limited Partnership Agreement and in this Offering Circular.

The term "production expenses" shall include fees of the director, choreographer, scenic, lighting and costume designers, orchestrator, cost of sets, curtains, drapes, costumes, properties, furnishings, electrical equipment, premiums for bonds and insurance, cash deposits with Actors' Equity Association or other similar organizations by which, according to customs or usual practices of theatrical business, such deposits may be required to be made, advances to the Author, rehearsal charges and expenses, transportation charges, cash office charges, reasonable legal and auditing expenses, advance publicity, theatre costs and expenses, and all other expenses and losses of whatever kind (other than expenditures precluded hereunder) actually incurred in connection with the production of the Play preliminary to the official opening of the Play. The General Partner has heretofore incurred or paid, and prior to the inception of the Partnership, will incur or pay, certain production expenses as herein set forth, and the amount thereof, and no more, shall be included in the production expenses of the Partnership, and (but only if all capital contributions for 50 Units shall have been received) the General Partner shall be reimbursed for the expenses so paid by him individually. The term "Running Expenses" shall mean all expenses, charges and disbursements of whatever kind actually incurred in connection with the operation of the Play, including without limiting the generality of the foregoing, royalties and/or other compensation to or for the Author, business and general managers, director, choreographer, orchestrator, cast stage help, transportation, cash office charge, reasonable legal and auditing expenses, theatre operating expenses, and all other expenses and losses of whatever kind actually incurred in connection with the operation of the Play, as well as taxes of whatever kind and nature other than taxes on the income of the respective Limited Partners and General Partner. Such Running Expenses shall include, without limitation, payments made in the form of Gross Receipts as well as participants in Net Profits to or for any of the aforementioned persons, services of rights.

The term "other expenses" shall be deemed to mean all expenses of whatsoever kind or nature other than those referred to in the two preceding paragraphs hereof actually and reasonably incurred in connection with the operation of the business of the Partnership, including, but without limiting the foregoing, commissions paid to agents, monies paid or payable in connection with claims for plagiarism, libel, negligence, etc.

As of the date of this Offering Circular, "Running Expenses" may be expected to include payment to the Author, General Partner, Designers and Director, amounting to eleven percent (11%) of the gross weekly box office receipts prior to recoupment of the total production costs and 13½% thereafter (if the Royalty Pool Formula becomes effective it will 5½% of such gross prior to recoupment and 14% thereafter). The Limited Partners' share of fifty percent (50%) of the net profits will accordingly be attributable to roughly 89% of the gross weekly box office receipts until such recoupment and 86½% thereafter except that if the Royalty Pool Formula becomes effective such 50% will be attributable to roughly 94½% of the gross weekly box office receipts till such recoupment and 86% thereafter. The producer has the right to further reduce the funds available for distribution by assigning a share of the net profits. There are no plans at the present time to assign any such share and if it does happen it will not exceed 5% of such net profits.

RETURN OF CAPITAL CONTRIBUTIONS— SHARE OF NET PROFITS

The Limited Partners as a group will be entitled to receive fifty percent (50%) of any net profits of the Partnership, each in the proportion which his capital contribution bears to the total capitalization of the Partnership. The General Partner will also receive fifty percent (50%) of such profits. Any net profits will be distributed only after all capital contributions have been returned to the Limited Partners and the Partnership maintains a reserve fund in the amount of $60,000.

Before net profits are earned, all losses will be borne by the Limited Partners to the extent of their respective capital contributions. After net profits are earned, the General Partner and Limited Partners will bear losses to the extent of the net profits in proportion to their respective interests. If the Partnership liabilities exceed its assets, all Partners, both General and Limited, will be required to return pro-rata any net profits distributed to them, and if a shortage remains, any repaid capital contributions as well. Even if the Play is successful, the Limited Partners may not have their capital contributions returned to them because the Limited Partnership Agreement provides that the General Partner may withhold net profits for investment in other productions of the Play without notice.

If repayment of capital contributions or distribution of Partnership net profits shall have been made prior or subsequent to the termination of the Partnership and, at any time thereafter, there shall be any unpaid debts, taxes, liabilities or obligations of the Partnership and the Partnership shall not have sufficient assets to meet the same, then the General Partner shall be entitled to recall all or part of the returned capital contributions and distributed Partnership net profits, in such aggregate amounts and under such circumstances as the General Partner deems necessary or advisable. Returned capital contributions will not be recalled until all Partnership net profits distributed to the General Partner and the Limited Partners have been recalled. If returned capital contributions are recalled, such recall shall be made ratably from all Limited Partners based upon their respective capital contributions to the Partnership, or in the case of Limited Partners who have posted bonds in lieu of making cash contributions, withdrawn ratably from the special bank accounts in which amounts equivalent to the repayment of capital contributions are to be deposited on their behalf. If distributed net profits are to be recalled, such recall shall be made from the General Partner and the Limited Partners in the same proportions as they shared in the distribution of such net profits.

Payments by the Limited Partners of recalled amounts are to be made within ten (10) days after receipt by each Limited Partner of the General Partner's written request therefor. If a Limited Partner does not return his share of distributed net profits or returned capital contributions when due, the remaining Limited Partners shall be liable (on a ratable basis dependent upon their respective capital contributions to the Partnership) for any defaulted amounts, but in no event shall such obligation of any non-defaulting Limited Partner exceed the amount of Partnership net profits theretofore distributed to the Limited Partner and capital contributions theretofore returned to the Limited Partner and not recalled from the Limited Partner. Any residual liabilities of the Partnership must be borne by the General Partner or any other persons who may agree to bear such liabilities.

OTHER FINANCING

Except as described above, no person or entity has advanced anything of value toward the production of the Play.

FINANCIAL STATEMENTS

The ultimate issuer of these securities will be the Partnership to be formed. Accordingly, no financial statements are presently available. Limited Partners will be furnished with all financial statements required by the New York Arts and Cultural Affairs Law and the Regulations promulgated in accordance with New York law, and will include, after formation of the Partnership, annual statements of operations. In cases where a lengthy period elapses after the initial expenditure of subscribers' funds, financial statements may have to be furnished even before formation of the Partnership. If the General Partner is permitted to furnish an unaudited statement, Limited Partners will not have the benefit of an accountant and will rely wholly upon the General Partner's statement for the determination of their share in any net profits.

EFFECT OF FEDERAL INCOME TAXES

It is the belief of the General Partner, that for purposes of federal income tax, the Partnership should be treated as a partnership. A tax ruling from the Internal Revenue Service as to the Partnership's status as a partnership for federal income tax purposes has not, however, been applied for, nor does the General Partner intend to apply for such a ruling. If the Partnership is treated as a partnership for federal income tax purposes, then: (a) the Partnership will be required to file an annual information tax return but will not itself be subject to federal income tax, and (b) each Limited Partner, regardless of whether he receives any distribution from the Partnership, will be required to report his proportionate share of each item of Partnership income and will be entitled to deduct (to the extent of his basis in his Limited Partnership Interest in the Partnership) and subject to the provisions of §469 of the Internal Revenue Code of 1986 as amended such proportionate share of each item of Partnership expense on the appropriate tax return of such Limited Partner for each relevant tax period.

LEGAL OPINIONS

Tanner Propp Fersko & Sterner, whose offices are located at 99 Park Avenue, New York, New York 10016, will act as counsel for the Partnership.

INDEMNIFICATION

There is no provision in the Limited Partnership Agreement or any contract, arrangement or statute under which any General Partner is insured or indemnified in any manner against any liability which he may incur in his capacity as such.

FEDERAL SECURITIES LAW

This offering of securities has been organized with the intent of qualifying for an exemption from the registration requirements of the Securities Act of 1933 (the "Act"), as amended, pursuant to Regulation A promulgated by the Securities and Exchange Commission under the Act. These securities are not registered under the Act. Whether these securities are exempt from registration pursuant to Regulation A or otherwise, has not been passed upon by the Securities and Exchange Commission, the Attorney General of the State of New York or any other regulatory agency, nor has any such agency passed upon the merits of this offering. The securities offered hereunder may not be resold without registration under the Act or exemption therefrom.

Appendix E

Budget for a Middle Theatre

"OTHER PEOPLE'S MONEY"

PROPOSED PRODUCTION BUDGET
FOR 399 SEAT OFF-BROADWAY THEATRE
ESTIMATED PRE-OPENING EXPENSES
3 WEEKS REHEARSAL
2 WEEKS PREVIEWS

PHYSICAL PRODUCTION

Scenery (Build, Paint, Flameproof)	$12,000	
Furniture, Props, Set Dressing	3,500	
Drapes, Curtains, Masking	2,000	
Costumes & Accessories	8,000	
Electric—Rental	4,000	
Electric Supplies	1,500	
Sound Equipment—Rental	500	
Put-In Crew	4,000	
Shop Prep & Work Calls	1,500	
Stage Preparation & Rigging	500	
Carting & Trucking	500	
		$38,000

REHEARSAL AND PREVIEW SALARIES

Cast	12,250	
Run-of-Play Payments	500	
Understudies	4,410	

Stage Manager	3,540
Asst. S.M./Understudy	2,700
Overscale payments	0
AEA Vacation Pay Accrual	935
Props/Carpenter (Rehearsals)	640
Electrician (Rehearsals)	720
Wardrobe—Supervisor	800
Crew Overtime (Reh. & Prev.))	1,440
General Manager	5,950
Company Manager	4,140
Press Agent	4,140
Production Secretary	0
Production Assistant	1,750
Attorney (Previews)	400
Accountant (Previews)	700
Box Office—Preliminary	1,600
House Staff—Preliminary	1,500
Ushers (Previews)	1,000

49,115

FEES

Director	5,125
Set Designer	3,000
Costume Designer	3,000
Lighting Designer	2,000
Sound Designer	0
Production Manager	2,000
Producer	0
General Manager	5,500
Attorney	7,500
Accountant	3,500
Casting Director	1,500
Asst's to Designers (S-2/C-2/L-3)	3,220

36,345

PROMOTION, PUBLICITY AND ADVERTISING

Newspaper Advertising (17.5K/7.5K/5K)	30,000
Media Advertising—Radio/TV	13,500
Mechanicals & Prep.	3,000
Window Cards	1,000
Flyers & Distribution	1,000
Marquees, Signs, Boards, Lobby, Etc.	3,000
Photographs	1,000

Press Agent Expenses	2,000	
Group Sales	500	
		55,000

ADMINISTRATIVE AND GENERAL
Scripts	1,000	
Casting & Auditions	2,000	
League Fee	60	
Rehearsal Halls	3,000	
Theatre Rent (Set-Up & Rehearsals)	3,500	
Theatre Rent (Previews)	12,000	
Theatre Service Package	6,200	
Theatre Expenses Thru Previews	3,450	
Producers Office Expense	3,150	
Gen. Mgr. Office Expense	1,750	
Tickets	900	
Program Expenses	350	
Union Pensions	3,635	
Union Health Insurance	3,835	
Payroll Taxes	8,590	
Business Taxes	930	
Computer Payroll & Checks	555	
Insurance - Production Package Deposit	4,000	
- Errors & Omissions	5,000	
- Per Capita Liability (Previews)	1,245	
Legal Disbursements	500	
Developmental Expenses	10,000	
Opening Night Expenses	3,500	
Departmental Expenses	1,000	
Miscellaneous	4,075	
		84,225

TOTAL ESTIMATED DIRECT PRODUCTION COSTS	$262,685

ADVANCES (NON-RETURNABLE)
Author	2,500	
Director	1,375	
Theatre	18,000	
		21,875

TOTAL ESTIMATED PRODUCTION COSTS WITH ADVANCES	$284,560

BONDS AND DEPOSITS (RETURNABLE)
AEA Bond	12,700	
ATPAM Bond	3,740	
Theatre Deposit	6,000	
		22,440

TOTAL ESTIMATED PRODUCTION DISBURSEMENTS $307,000

RESERVES [Not Including Preview Income]
General Reserve	15,000	
Reserve for Post Opening Advertising Support	18,000	
		33,000

TOTAL ESTIMATED PRODUCTION CAPITALIZATION $340,000

* *

SUBSCRIPTION BASED ON CAPITALIZATION ABOVE

EACH OF FIFTY (50) "UNITS": $6,800

* *

"OTHER PEOPLE'S MONEY"

ESTIMATED WEEKLY OPERATING EXPENSES
FOR 399 SEAT OFF-BROADWAY THEATRE
BASED ON GROSS OF $40,000

SALARIES AND FEES
Cast	$2,500
Run-of-Play Payments	250
Understudies	1,500
Stage Manager	610
Asst. S.M./Understudy	555
AEA Vacation & Sick Pay Accrual	385
Prop/Carpenter	320
Electrician	360
Wardrobe—Supervisor	320
General Manager	850
Company Manager	690
Press Agent	690
Attorney	200
Accountant	350

Casting	150	
Designers	300	
		$10,030

ADVERTISING AND PUBLICITY

Newspaper Advertising	6,000	
Media Advertising—Radio	1,000	
Press Agent Expenses	200	
Flyers and Distribution	200	
		7,400

ADMINISTRATIVE AND GENERAL

Tickets	165	
Program Maintenance, Inserts, Etc.	20	
Producer Office Expense	450	
Gen. Mgr. Office Expense	250	
Union Pensions	635	
Union Health Insurance	765	
Payroll Taxes	1,310	
Business Taxes	480	
Computer Payroll & Checks	55	
Insurance (Prod. $300 + P/C @ $.41/per head)	1,150	
Rentals - Electrics	875	
- Sound	50	
Costume Cleaning & Ward. Dept. Exp.	75	
Departmental Expenses	50	
Miscellaneous	140	
		6,470

THEATRE RENT AND EXPENSES

Rental Guarantee	6,000	
Service Package	3,100	
Utilities, Air Conditioning, Etc.	1,000	
		10,100

TOTAL ESTIMATED FIXED OPERATING EXPENSES $34,000

ROYALTIES AND PERCENTAGES	At Gross	$40,000
Author	- 5.0%	2,000
Director	- 2.0%	800
Producer	- 2.0%	800
Original Production Company	- 1.0%	400

TOTAL ROYALTIES   - 10.0%   4,000
Theatre Percentage Participation
    5% of Gross from 1st Dollar   2,000
                                                                6,000

BREAK EVEN:
TOTAL ESTIMATED WEEKLY RUNNING EXPENSE
BASED ON A GROSS OF $40,000 $40,000
* *
* *

RECAP
[with $25 Average Ticket and Standard Royalties Paid]

MAXIMUM POTENTIAL WEEKLY GROSS AT 399 SEAT
    HOUSE $79,800

ESTIMATED WEEKLY EXPENSE AT MAXIMUM $49,600

ESTIMATED WEEKLY PROFIT AT MAXIMUM $30,200

AT CAPACITY, IT WOULD TAKE 11.26 WEEKS TO REPAY $340,000.
    BREAK EVEN POINT: 50.13% OF ESTIMATED CAPACITY
* *